ON THE MARGINS
U.S. Americans in
a border town to Mexico

Johannes Wilm

Dedicated to the lumpenproletariat, without whom a world revolution
will never be possible

Lulu Enterprises, Inc.

Published by Lulu Enterprises, Inc.
3131 RDU Center, Suite 210
Morrisville, NC 27560
www.lulu.com

The Library of Congress has cataloged the first edition as follows:
Wilm, Johannes, 1980-
    On the margins : U.S. Americans in a border town to Mexico /
Johannes Wilm.
        xiv, 219 p. : ill. ; 23 cm.
    Includes bibliographical references (p. 215-219).
    LCCN 2005910888
    ISBN-10: 1-4116-6175-3 (pbk.)
    ISBN-13: 978-1-4116-6175-2 (pbk.)
1. Douglas (Ariz.)–Social conditions. 2. Marginality,
Social–Arizona–Douglas. I. Title.
HN80.D68W55 2005
                                                    14291752

Preface

I first came to Douglas in early 2004 to do field research for my master thesis. However, during my time in Douglas, I learned much more than a Norwegian master's thesis in 2005 could possibly contain. Also, the academic degree structure in Norway had recently changed starting in the fall of 2003, so no one knew what a master's thesis should contain. Unfortunately, my fellow students and I found out that the formal requirements, which were previously flexible, now had to be met to the letter, and that they really were serious about European standardization this time. This will convert much of the university into little more than a school — changing the emphasis from free studies to recital of "known and proven" facts. It reminds me of the following quote from the beginning of the doctor thesis of Marx:

> The form of this treatise would have been on the one hand more strictly scientific, on the other hand in many of its arguments less pedantic, if its primary purpose had not been that of a doctor's dissertation. I am nevertheless constrained by external reasons to send it to the press in this form. Moreover I believe that I have solved in it a heretofore unsolved problem in the history of Greek philosophy. (Marx 1841)

It seems as though some capitalists finally have discovered knowledge itself as a market to profit from. Learning is rapidly transformed into something having product-like qualities, such as consisting of a measurable quantity and having a fixed and comparable price in a free market. The same process is increasingly being viewed as an economic investment that will pay out in the form of a higher salary upon gaining a degree. All that is independent of the relevance of the insight one has gained during the research.

Fortunately, I felt encouraged by several people and found the time to write this ethnography — of which I handed in roughly one third as my thesis.

Oslo, December 2005

Acknowledgment

I want to thank all those, who helped me in some way during both the writing and the empirical research. In particular, I would like to thank Oscar Alvarado, Sarah Austin, Cesar Avitia, Glenda, Joseph and Stuart Bavier, David Caveny, Mike Fallwell, Curtis Foster, Hunt Hoffman, Carolina Langham, Annie Mora, Shaine Parker, Adrian Pedrego, Irma Perez, Larry Reed and Keoki Skinner for their extraordinary help in getting me into contact with an enormously high number of people in Douglas, as well as engaging in discussions on an ever-changing range of topics. Back home I was surprised by and thankful to Marianne Sun May Per and Francis Rønnestad for their many hours of reading and commenting on my writings. Also, I would like to thank Wiebke Bleicken, Jan Willi Christiansen, Sara Cools, Helle Gabler, Christopher Gambert, Aksel Gihle, Mustafa Hussain, Lena Jessen, Benjamin Jonsrud, Marthe Høyer, Mats Mago Isaksen, Trond Klykken, Marielle Leraand, Heidi Lundeberg, Sigrid Steffensen Melkeraaen, Anne May Melsom, Harald Nicolaisen, Niels Søndergård Nielsen, Marte Nilsen, Barbara Paech, Sjur Cappelen Papazian, Tormod Friis Pettersen, Cornelia Schöler, Rolf Solvang, Linus Strothmann, Erlend Torp and Beret Werner as well as my grandmothers Anne-Marie Wilm and Joyce Nissen, my parents Pia and Gero and my siblings Julius, Jakob and Jensine Wilm. I thank them for their comments, and mental support during various stages of the writing, and general help with some of my other concurrent projects to still give me time to write. In addition, I wish to thank all for broadening my horizon enough to make this study possible to begin with.

I also want to thank my adviser Thomas Hylland Eriksen for the help in finding relevant literature and structuring it properly, and Edwin M. Basye for his thorough editing services.

Contents

Preface iii

Acknowledgment iv

Introduction   **1**

Anthropological views of the borderland 3

Marxist Anthropology 4

    Practice 6

Information 9

The community 11

Going to Douglas 12

1 Places   **15**

The pasta crisis — social life at the Lerman 17

    Getting to know one another 17

    Social Life 19

    The "not so socials" 23

Chatting at El Espejo 24

Checking out girls at the library 26

    The Douglas Cultural Elite 28

    The Lerman residents gone bookish 29

Ghetto people at La Gardin 30

Games at 10th Street Park 33

Living history at the Douglas Wendt house 35

Fascists at the gun shop 37

Cross-spatial events 38

    John's good-bye reception 38

    The drug war 40

    The election 41

Conclusion 43

2 **Money** **45**
Mr. Fernandez 47
John 49
Art 55
Zack 57
Joe 60
Todd 61
Bruce 63
Soerlie 65
Sarah and Tom 69
Bicycle Peter 71
Garry Mora 74
Maria 75
Jeff and January 76
Conclusion 77
Class 77
Economic constructions of community 78

3 **Crossing the line** **79**
Physical Border 81
Shopping the hard way 81
The prostitute 82
Zack physical 84
Bruce and The Physical Border 86
Winter Visitors 88
Local Youngsters 91
Peter's first time 93
Language Boundary 95
Oscar, first Hispanic president 95
Bruce, rock worker 96
Todd, more than Mexican 96
Cultural Barrier 97
John socializing 98
Bruce goes to Tucson 101
Peter living in the United States 103
The trailer park 105

Art & Tom 109
Todd crossing without crossing 110
Jeff staying where he is 112
Kevin, the borderless 113
Conclusion 114
Ideas about Mexico 115
Historical Aspects 115
Material Reasons for Persistence of the Border . . . 116
Particular features 117

4 Crime   119
The Structuralist View 119
The Political-Economical View 121
Crime in borderlands 122
John's got a gun 123
Petty Crimes 129
The Social Security Scam 130
Registering Cars 130
Street kids 132
Registering Foreign Voters 134
Copying Music 138
Final Analysis 139
Conclusion 140

5 War & Nationalism   145
The recruiter 146
Douglas graduates 147
War is Over 153
The Anti-Nationals 153
Foreign but Nationalist 156
U.S. American Nationalist 156
Do soldiers have the same function as proletarians? . . . 159

6 Douglas and the World   163
Douglas connected to the United States 163
Connection through comparability 164
Connection through interdependence 166
Douglas disconnected from the United States 167

Agents from the outside 169
Law Enforcement 172
Hiding from the government 174
Conclusion 175

Conclusion   **177**
Class 178
The Importance of Structure 180
A prophetic value? 182
Social stratification 182
The times, they are changing? 183
Action? 184
Problems 184
Positive factors 185

A People   **187**
Mr. Fernandez 187
John 188
Leaving Town 191
Angel 191
Zack 192
Tom 193
Oscar 194
Cosmic Peter 195
Edwin Ludszeweit 196
Maria & her crew 197
Art 200
Stan 202
Todd 203
Kevin 205
Garry Mora 206
Bicycle Peter 206
Sgt. Skinner 208

B History, Terms, Tools & Problems   **209**
History 209
Terminology 211

The idea of a dual notion of nationalism under capitalism 212
The concept of citizenship 212
The term 'lumpenproletariat' 214
Theoretical Tools 215
Problematic Issues 217
Sample 217
Time slices 219

Bibliography   **220**

Pictures

1   'Pray for Douglas — Miracles still happen" — a sign in downtown Douglas.   x
2   The pool is one of few public employment opportunities.   2
3   The broad streets of Douglas were created for street carts.   3
4   The Douglas library was the place to meet people. .   14
5   The TV was the main meeting spot at the Posada Lerman.   14
6   Inside the El Espejo kitchen   24
7   John got a free juice at El Espejo.   50
8   Art and the telescope that will save the Douglas economy. Picture taken at a shelter in New Mexico, Art's car is in the background.   54
9   Bicycle Peter in his trailer in the United States   71
10   Douglas and AP youngsters in an ethnicised show of Mexican culture — mostly for rich golf tourists? .   98
11   The rock working crew only speaks Spanish. Todd is the exception.   111
12   Prisoners working on Douglas downtown roads . .   120
13   The Douglas border entrance. Fire arms are 'forbidden' in Mexico.   141
14   This is a happy day. Douglas soldiers have returned from Iraq.   148
15   Children in a parade celebrating Douglas soldiers .   148

Picture 1: 'Pray for Douglas — Miracles still happen" — a sign in downtown Douglas.

16   Shopping opportunities in Douglas are limited. . . . 167
17   Border Patrol trying to recruit youngsters with an
     information booth 172
18   Joe's self built house is energy efficient and not con-
     nected to the main grid. 175
19   Luis hopes he has found life-time job in the Douglas
     fire brigade. 179
20   Returning soldiers from Iraq during a parade 180
21   Tom and Sarah in the July 4th parade 193
22   Kids playing soccer on the parking lot in front of
     Todd's house and behind La Gardin 204
23   Douglas is still wealthy compared to Agua Prieta. . 207
24   Douglas' low altitude made it the perfect location
     for a smelter. 210
25   A closed down business — one of many 211
26   Collection for veterans during the annual "Arts in
     the Park" 212
27   The new Wal-Mart Superstore is the subject of many
     conversations. 216
28   The area where the Barkers live is somewhat wealthier.218
29   A few chain stores have been established west of town.226
30   A few miles outside of Douglas, the border fence
     suddenly ends. 226

Introduction

D
OUGLAS was a small, but growing city when I conducted this study in 2004. At the time, it had a population of 16,740 (of Commerce Communications Division 2005); while in 2000 it had only had 14,312 inhabitants (Census 2000). The inmates at the prison comprised about 2,000 of that population. Without any real employment available, 75% of the school children were eligible for reduced lunches at the school cafeteria — a figure the librarian used when she applied for a free T1 Internet line for the library. About 53% of those under 18 years old were officially living under the poverty line (Census 2000). Besides the library, there were a few middle schools, one high school, a nearby college that Douglas shared with its neighboring town Bisbee, a few classrooms connected to the University of Arizona, a radio station, an outdoor pool, an Aquatic Center, a daily newspaper, a famous old hotel with an impressive lobby and not so impressive rooms, a Motel 6 and few other budget motels, a handful of gas stations, a grocery store for the poor called Food City, a grocery store for the relatively wealthy called Safeway, a Wal-Mart, the prison with its 2000 inmates, a small inner city filled mostly with various kinds of dollar stores run by Koreans, and "the worlds largest border station," as a Douglasite woman told me.

Phelps Dodge founded the city in 1901 to host a copper smelter. The smelter closed in the 1980s. It led to the mostly Anglo management moving out of town to their new headquarters in Phoenix, while the smelter itself moved south into Mexico to save labor costs. The blue-collar, mostly Hispanic workers stayed in Douglas. In addition, the *North American Free Trade Agreement* (NAFTA) has led to an enormous increase in people trying to cross the border from

1

Photo: Johannes Wilm

Picture 2: The pool is one of few public employment opportunities.

Mexico to the U.S. .

Since then, smuggling people and drugs has been the main source of income for the town. In the year 2000, the border patrol arrested 289,200 'illegal' immigrants (Zaragoza 2000), and according the local border patrol agents I spoke to, they catch about one in five, which would mean that about 1.5 million 'illegal aliens' pass through Douglas yearly. George Magazine had an article on America's ten most corrupt cities in 1998. The list included Douglas, AZ, as well as Chester, PA; Clovis, CA; Alek Providence, LA; Youngstown, OH; Eastman, GA; Kansas City, MO; Las Vegas, Nevada; Miami, FL; and Washington D.C. (Offman 1998). The mayor William Dell spent most of his time around Food City, and rumors had it that he got a salary from them. Although such information was likely to be on the public record, a Douglas woman told me "you don't want to be researching that too much cause you do not know what will happen to you."

Because some of the information I gained during my stay is sensitive, I decided to change all the names of individuals for

Photo: Johannes Wilm

Picture 3: The broad streets of Douglas were created for street carts.

their privacy. I also changed the names of the often mentioned establishments. However, the names of Douglas and other towns are real — the city of Douglas does exist. To all who read this work and get fascinated with all the different groups and individuals who are living in Douglas, I recommend that they visit Douglas. And know that the groups that I have described here are only one tiny portion of Douglas, so with all likelihood, your experience will significantly differ from mine. But be aware, the slogan of Douglas is: "Come for a Day, Stay for a Lifetime!" — and you have to take that as a prophecy.

Anthropological views of the borderland

Robert Alvarez Jr. divides the period after WWII, which marks the start of studies of the areas around the border, into several schools. During the 1950s and 1960s, researchers mostly saw border area as an isolated area, as the border demarcated the end of a cultural space. In the heyday of modernization theory, one of the major studies concerned itself with Mexican culture as a hindrance to the delivery of U.S. health-care. However, researchers were not interested in the border itself. When the population in the area increased during the 1980s, researchers finally became interested in the border. In the 1990s, many studies of the border focus on various policies affecting the border. These included the heightened degree of law enforcement, Mexican migrants, or the growing presence of maquiladora factories on the Mexican side of the border. (Alvarez 1995, 452)

Even more recently, Hastings Donnan and Thomas M. Wilson try to look at borderlands and how anthropologists are studying them today (Donnan and Wilson 1999). While anthropologists still study the U.S.-Mexican borderland a lot, they also are studying other borderlands. Their analysis puts a greater emphasis on the special place economics have in borderlands in general, and how people living near a border are being marginalized both economically and geographically.

Also I will in the following chapters look at the economics of Douglas and I do not take 'culture' much into consideration. But in contrast to other current anthropologists, I will build on a Marxist understanding of economics.

Anthropological genre — Marxist Anthropology

I look at sociology and politics from a Marxist viewpoint and, given my anthropological method, I therefore work within Marxist Anthropology. Combining Marxism and anthropology has had many different proponents, both in European and North American Anthropology in the post-WWII era. Most recently, Marcus and Menzies have contributed by starting the journal *New Proposals* and editing an issue of the Canadian-based journal *Anthropologica*. But what does 'Marxist Anthropology' mean in practical terms?

William Roseberry (1997a, 307) tries to define this exact term, but the only definition he can give is simply that the writer combines some Marxist theory with anthropology. He goes on to try to establish three main branches of themes taken up by Marxist anthropologists: 'materialism,' 'social evolution' and 'capitalism.'

'Materialism' deals with the need to understand the mode of production in a society to understand the 'social whole' or political and cultural superstructure of society (Roseberry 1997a, 307). Roseberry condemns this approach as useless because he believes that the base and the superstructure cannot be separated in an anthropological study (Roseberry 1997a).

In contrast, according to the way Bridget O'Laughlin argues for creating a historical materialist anthropological perspective, one can build on a philosophy of dialectic materialism by simply accepting interplay between ideology and material reality, in which the material reality will be the decisive factor in the end (O'Laughlin 1975, 341–342). Therefore one does not need to classify each individual case according to whether it belongs to base or super structure. Also, in reality, some things such as income level and legally defined ownership over means of production are closer to the base of society than others, such as one's taste in music or a preference for political ideology. Furthermore, Roseberry's definition of 'society' seems to be static. As O'Laughlin (1975, 346–348) points out: Marx sees production as a process for social change. That is why the borders of a 'society' have to be explained and cannot be taken for granted. They will constantly change as well, just as the production process does. Therefore, for anthropologists, one interesting aspect is to see how human life flexibly adapts to the conditions it finds at any point of time (O'Laughlin 1975, 346–348). Second, in the case of 21st century capitalism, full-scale autarchic societies might not even exist at a world level.

'Social evolution' provides several approaches for integrating different 'pre-capitalist societies' in a Marxist analysis in which the mode of production is taken as the defining factor for the rest of society (Roseberry 1997a, 308–309).

Also in Douglas, and even more so in Agua Prieta, a large percentage of the social and productive organization follows pre-capitalist principles (large family networks that work as economic and productive entities). But the number of DVD-players and fancy pick-up trucks is way too high for it all to be counted as (part of) a pre-capitalist society.

It is within the third field of Marxist anthropology, the study of 'capitalism,' that most of this thesis has to be placed. Roseberry

mainly classifies texts that look at the expansion of capitalist relationships in pre-capitalist societies (Roseberry 1997a, 309) into this
category. But also texts like this one written after the decline of
employment, which has been occurring since the oil crisis and has
led to a decline in capitalist relationships, especially in places like
Douglas, should be able to fit into this category.

The important point to remember is that Marxist anthropology
does not represent merely one single line of thought, but is an
opening for a whole range of possible anthropological approaches
that have a common basis in the writings of Marx.

Practice

> The philosophers have only *interpreted* the world, in
> various ways; the point is to *change* it.(Engels and Marx
> 1974, XI. Theses on Feuerbach, 123)

One of the most controversial issues amongst Marxists is what
aim one should have as a scientist. While Roseberry approves of
certain aspects of the analytical tools given by Marx (for academic
purposes), he thoroughly condemns using Marx theories as a basis
on which to found a program for change. This is known among
Marxists as 'practice' — the combination of studying and acting
upon what is learned. According to Roseberry (1997b, 25, 43–44),
all such approaches have a positivist flavor, and most previous
attempts to try to alter history according to a Marxist scheme have
since been discredited. In contrast, O'Laughlin (1975, 342) argues
that research in itself or earning academic degrees cannot be the
primary aim of Marxists. Rather, the aim of research must be to
prepare oneself well to change the world for the better, and because
of the interplay between the world of ideas and material facts,
this has to be manifested in physical actions; no situation can be
completely deconstructed on paper.

The difference between the theoretical and the practical Marxist
does not always have to be as clearly delineated as it is between
O'Laughlin and Roseberry, who openly states his disgust with the
XI. *Theses on Feuerbach* (Roseberry 1997b, 25). Rather, as Marcus
and Menzies (2005b, 17) conclude about Marxist anthropologists

of the late 1960's era, almost all of them lay somewhere between the activist and the theoretician, and the issues of conflict are well-known.

Marcus and Menzies call for a return to a more activist anthropological practice with the stated goal of "achieving a classless society" and getting there by using the communication channels that are open to anthropologists (Marcus and Menzies 2005b, 14, 26). The reason why they believe it is possible for Marxists to speak openly today is not because they have great faith in the Seattle 99 *globalization-from-below*-movement[1] nor that they have great faith in a great coming global upsurge of rebellion that is imperative because of higher rates of economic exploitation, the way some read Marx (Boswell and Dixon 1993). Rather it is because one can notice a renewed belief in bourgeois rule amongst the establishment (Marcus and Menzies 2005a; Marcus and Menzies 2005b). That is why those in power are not as repressive towards people expressing revolutionary ideas, or even those planning and conducting large strikes in the major capitals of Europe, as was commonplace at one time (Marcus and Menzies 2005b, 22).

I have more faith than Marcus and Menzies in the long-term effects of the *globalization-from-below*-movement, through whose European wing I became a socialist myself, but I entirely agree with the two regarding the need for more activism — or practice. Now, I did not start a revolution in Douglas, but I freely allowed myself to discuss politics on interpersonal, local and global issues with my information sources, at least to the degree it felt appropriate. In many ways, that is as much as I could have hoped for.

Although we might have different outlooks on the strength and progressive character of the current movements, I also completely agree with Marcus and Menzies that the new world order which followed the cold war has ended the stalemate in the struggle between capital and labor, and that the wars conducted by the United States and the United Kingdom, as well as the rearmament of the European powers and Japan, are clear signs that we have come into an "age of war, consolidation, and crisis for the world capitalist system." And crises are, according to Wolf, periods of

---

[1]A global movement of decentralized activism that came into existence following the shutdown of the 1999 WTO Congress in Seattle, Washington.

time when people's imaginations seem to run wild — Marxist ideas might once more have a chance of getting more generally accepted. (Marcus and Menzies 2005b, 23)

The work that first inspired me to conduct the study was Barbara Ehrenreich's *Nickel and Dimed*, a study of the working poor in various American towns. She uses classical field work methods by attempting to live the same way that her informants do and she also frequently considered to what extent she should be documenting and to what degree she should be trying to make a difference right there and then. She also bases her post-post-modern analysis almost exclusively on theory from the original writings of Marx (Ehrenreich 2002). However, my study of Douglas produced quite a different result — both because I studied a different segment of the U.S. population, and because I had a totally different status among my informants; while she was an older American PhD hiding her educational status at various low-wage jobs in areas with long driving distances, I was a foreign youth focused on much smaller geographical area, I started with nearly no social connections in the U.S. other than the informants, and I spent most of my time walking around a town that I did not need a car for.

In contrast to both Ehrenreich and Marcus, I believe that what I observed was mostly the lumpenproletariat (the unemployed) rather than the proletariat (the workers). In the case of Ehrenreich, it is because she is mostly looking at people with jobs — the working poor, while the case of Marcus has more to do with how we classify people. Marcus (2005) conducted a study of 'the homeless' in New York City in the 1990's, through which he concluded that no one had homelessness as his or her only problem, and that the need for a place to sleep must be seen as just one of several needs that the poorer segments of what he calls 'the working class' cannot always fulfill. In terms of income and activity, the people he looks at are not so different from my informants, and therefore I have wondered why we differed in the way we labeled them. One explanation might be that Marxists were not always so positive towards the lumpenproletariat (see — "The term 'lumpenproletariat'", p. 214), and that he does not see the need for addressing that issue. In contrast, I bring the discussion here, and I hope to show that these people cannot simply be ignored.

Information

I gathered information from many different people at various places in Douglas. The following gives a short overview of how this worked.

During my stay in Douglas I lived at three different locations. These locations are distinguishable by the class background of those living there.

First, I stayed in the downtown Posada Lerman. It was a place known in Douglas for its type of tenants, which came to the Lerman either directly out of jail or had other major economic and social problems. It also probably had one of the highest tenant turnovers of any place in town, and yet most of those tenants had a long-term connection with Douglas, in contrast to those staying at the Motel 6, for example. My co-tenants were all men, roughly between the ages of 30 and 70. I concluded after moving out that it was the need for mutual help in finding jobs, trading food stamps, finding free food at churches, preparing food together, and social interaction to combat the general sense of loneliness that brought these people together. Although I did move out after only a month's stay at the Posada Lerman, I did stay in contact with nearly all the tenants. I was always a frequent visitor, although to varying degrees at different times, for the rest of my stay. This allowed me to record some changes in the life of several of the Lerman residents, although many of these changes were quite minor.

The second place I stayed at was the house of Todd Daniels, an LA Times Reporter in Vietnam during the war, who also was a temporary editor for the Douglas newspaper The Daily Dispatch in the late eighties. Todd then lived in South America for most of the nineties before coming back to Douglas late in that decade, where he began to smuggle 'illegal' immigrants across the border. He was caught for these activities in 2001 and had gone to prison for 18 months, but then returned to Douglas to sit out his probation period. He had a downtown house (without furniture), which he had bought for the money he had made smuggling and now was eagerly trying to sell, so he could pay off his fine to gain the freedom to leave the U.S. again. Todd had a job that paid him 10 USD a day at the juice bar El Espejo owned by his good friend

Kevin Russ, who also made very little money. Although Todd had no more money than the inhabitants of the Posada Lerman had, he had two college degrees and was generally counted as part of the 'cultural elite' of Douglas. Therefore, he had more possibilities to be influential in Douglas. My second set of data therefore was focused around the El Espejo and the small group of people who hung around it a lot. They were largely distinguished by having a higher education than most other people in Douglas.

The third place I lived at was the librarian's house. She lived with her retired husband and during my stay there, with her son, who had recently come back after seven years of studies across Europe to become a journalist. The family was in the same cultural elite category as Todd and Kevin, but they differed in that they had a higher income.

Nevertheless, all three groups either knew one another already or got to know one another during my time there. This was partially due to my movement between the groups, but several connections were also formed independently of my presence.

During my entire stay, the library was the main place I hung around, and with its Internet computers and air conditioner it was the main hangout for quite distinct groups of Douglasites who could not afford either one. From there, I developed long-term connections with two groups of high school graduates (one conservative and the other mainly lesbian), the Cyber Teens (a group of youngsters who maintained the computers in their spare time), a group of retired teachers, a telescope and airplane scientist who lived on the parking lot until we got him moved into the Lerman Hotel, a computer programmer from Santa Cruz who wanted to escape corporate America and develop a sustainable community outside Douglas, and an international expert on chicken genetics who felt he was German and who had been participating in bike races all across Europe when he was in the ARMY.

In addition to people in the library and other places mentioned above, I talked extensively to the gun shop owner and his co-worker, four couples of winter visitors from Canada and the Northern States that came to Douglas every winter, Juan (the city gardener), Monica and Arlie (who worked for the senior citizens coffee hour on Tuesdays and Thursdays), Monica's step father, one prisoner (who worked in the park regularly), Oscar (a former student council president at Douglas High School), Alexis Sanders (a contender for the elections of mayor), three people from the Douglas Historical Society, the owner of Douglas Coffee, the staff at the bakery La Gardin, Bicycle Peter (a senior citizen who lived in Mexico for most of my stay and had been living there most of his life), and Soerlie (a retired gay and communist music teacher from Texas who came in order to smoke crack in Mexico but had to leave after a few weeks when he could not get along with his neighbors).

The community

What kind of community might the Douglas inhabitants, the Douglasites, belong to? One could imagine that their community could be seen as being 'the town,' 'the state' or 'the country' as with any other town in the U.S. . But because it is Douglas, one could add to that 'Mexico,' 'the Mexican state of Sonora,' 'both countries' and a 'border community' that consists of people living in a stretch of land on both sides of the border. It seems obvious that the definition of 'community' one uses will largely determine the answer one will get.

I found three of the above positions in border literature:

Donnan and Wilson (1999) looks at the border people as subverting national regulations and laws, but ultimately as dependent on the exchange cycles of the two countries involved, and that is why they are careful not to subvert power of the states in a way that would result in revolutionary change.

Stern (2004) analyzes an earlier period (1910–1940), studying how the standardization of the border patrol along the border turned the U.S. side of border into a more homogenized area through the imposition of a system of rights and obligations that were linked to citizenship and therefore kept Mexicans out. This analysis still seems relevant today. At the same time, while some areas in the U.S. had an outstanding position that was recognized by everybody — like the quickly modernizing California — areas such as Arizona were merely parts of the country with no outstanding features. Although Stern writes about a certain period, Arizona

still does not have the outstanding features that California has —
even today, and so according to that logic, it would still have to be
seen as a rather nondescript part of the country.

Miller (2000) and Weisman (1986) focus on the border as an area
in itself. Through an extensive ethnographic study of people living
on both sides of the border along its entire length, Miller tries to
show that the borderland should be regarded as an area somewhat
independent of the two countries involved. Although not clearly
spelled out, his theory entails a view that Douglas and other border areas are not part of the 'world system'[2], but rather a local
space, somehow disconnected from everything. While Weisman
agrees in the theory of the borderland being a separate space of its
own, for him this has more to do with the interdependence that
is slowly growing across the border, and therefore the borderland
would eventually grow geographically into a space of intercultural
connectedness.

While all three of these positions have convincing arguments
and they all have valid points, they lack an analytical method and
instead depend on finding various examples that fit their initial
theory.

In order to take a serious analytical approach, I will try to show
that it makes sense to look a bit at the Marxist framework. Marx
does not give one clear answer about what constitutes a community
and consequently what community the people in Douglas are parts
of. Nevertheless, Marxism certainly lends us a few tools to be a bit
more systematic about approaching an answer to this question. In
the various chapters, I will try to use different ways that community
can be constructed, and see how much validity this particular
definition of community has, and how far it extends geographically.

Going to Douglas

I flew out of Hamburg on the sixth of January 2004 and entered the
U.S. via the Chicago O'Hare airport. The Polish officer handling

---

[2]The 'world system theory' is usually attributed to Immanuel Wallerstein,
which emphasizes the global nature of the production system in which developed
and undeveloped countries play different parts (Hall 1997, 498).

my entrance said I was "in the[ir] system" and I was to be put into a 'terrorist container' together with lots of other men, who had obviously been put there because they looked like Arabians. After a few minutes, my Polish officer waved over to me and gestured that I should follow him. He walked to another row of computers, and after typing a few things he announced that I was now deleted "from the[ir] system." He also told me, that he had done me a favor and that all the others had to wait at least three hours. My luggage that I was supposed to re-check-in was delayed, so I flew on to Tucson without it. The lady at the airport who was in charge of my luggage announced to everybody waiting in line that I was "to study rocks" when I told her I was going to Douglas to do my masters in anthropology. "I hope you get to see something else as well," she continued, "Arizona is a whole lot more than Douglas."

On my way to a motel in Tucson for one night before I was to go on to Douglas, I met three other students. One of them was studying at Harvard and was just there for an eco-conference. The other two, a Canadian girl and her Mexican boyfriend who had just come back from visiting her parents in Vancouver over Christmas, were studying in Tucson. When they heard what I was going to be doing, they offered me some contacts to pro-immigrant organizations, but I declined based on me wanting to obtain that information directly from Douglasites. Little was I to know how far I was going to be from academia for quite a while. After my night at the motel, I took a bus on to Douglas where I had reserved 4 nights at the local Motel 6 over the Internet.

For two months I had been trying to get a room in Douglas via the few apartment agencies that were listed on the Internet, but none of them had ever answered the phone except once, when they offered a room for 1000 USD/month, which was way outside my budget. As a last act of desperation, I had therefore booked into the Motel 6, at least for a few nights.

The first two days I spend walking up and down some of the downtown streets, trying to find phone numbers of real estate agencies. Then I saw the sign at the Posada Lerman and I walked right in. The old lobby of the hotel was closed, but there was a sign saying that the manager lived in number sixteen. I went to the door and knocked.

Photo: Johannes Wilm

Picture 4: The Douglas library was the place to meet people.

Photo: Johannes Wilm

Picture 5: The TV was the main meeting spot at the Posada Lerman.

Chapter 1

Places in the context of Class, Ethnicity and Language

A T first sight, Douglas is reminiscent of many other places
without jobs and a comprehensive welfare system —
there are a variety of downtown hangouts, and there
are quite a number of unemployed and semi-employed
people who spend most or a lot of their time going from place to
place and who hang around in various settings. Some people live
close by and hang out daily at many different places, while others
come from farther away and just show up at one or two of them
occasionally. What characterizes a number of the hangouts is that
they all are in within a few blocks and so one can easily walk
from one to another. But in Douglas, it is not quite as simple to
determine the pattern of where people go. As one would expect,
the different hangouts are somewhat differentiated according to
class/background. But what can the differences between these
various places tell us about ethnicity and language?

It is often claimed that the state requires differentiating space
according to ethnicity, among other things in order to keep hegemonic control; the dominant ethnicity is connected to the core of
the nation, while other ethnic groups are confined to the outskirts
of society (Alonso 1994, 394). If this is true, we would expect U.S.

American ethnicity to be connected to the most central parts of society, while Mexican culture would be expected to be on the outskirts. One of the frequent points of migration studies is the existence of non-nationalized pockets within the territorial boundaries of the United States in which social-cultural patterns, rather than the geographic location, define the nationality. (Alvarez 1995, 457)

Thinking in a similar vein, but within a rather different framework, the anti-immigration activist Samuel P. Huntington tries to give a historic overview of the United States and to determine to what extent the national identity included ethnicity. Initially among the 17th and 18th century settlers, which were mainly white, Protestant, and British, the U.S. was defined as a combination of race, ethnicity, culture, and religion. When ties were cut to Britain, an ideological dimension was added to this. With more immigration coming from other parts of Europe at the end of the 19th century, the definition of the ethnic base of the U.S. was expanded to also include Scandinavian, German and Irish elements. But with the arrival of the Second World War, which drove many East Europeans to the United States, and then the Civil Rights Movement, which more fully included African Americans into the United States nation, ethnicity and race generally stopped being a part of the definition of the U.S. nation. Huntington states that instead of a specific ethnicity, those who hold United States citizenship see their nation as multi-ethnic and multiracial. However, in recent years, the United States is being threatened with being divided by language and culture, as a result of the heavy influx of Hispanic and especially Mexican immigrants; he believes that the divide between Anglos and Hispanics might replace the earlier divide between blacks and whites. The main reason why they will not be absorbed into American mainstream culture is that the close proximity of Mexico means that they do not have to assimilate. This sounds very similar to Alvarez' concept of cultural non-nationalized pockets, but Huntington sees it mainly as a threat against the existence of a general national identity and way of life. (Huntington 2004)

Let us follow these threads of thought and while looking at the various publicly accessible places around Douglas, noticing to what extent they serve as national homogenized spaces that serve in a hegemonic way to further U.S. nationalism.

The pasta crisis — social life at the Lerman

The Posada Lerman or Lerman Hotel is the first place I stay at. You can read about some of the main characters at the Lerman in Appendix A, but they describe themselves well when they speak of one another as "not having all their noodles together." At the Posada Lerman, everyone is known as a number corresponding to the room number, which I believe is used primarily to communicate easily across language barriers. The tenants there are very transient, but when I visit increasingly more often about four months after leaving, the numbering system still is the same, although the general level of communication has declined to the point that coordinating the use of the common phone is almost the only subject of discussion. The phone is located in the lobby together with the sofa, the TV, and the heater. When coming back to Douglas for my second stay, I stay at the Lerman the entire time. The phone and TV are still the same, but the heater is not longer working.

Some of the tenants of the Lerman are 'hobos,' in that they have traveled from a long way and used to have a stable family somewhere else (Anderson 1923, 138). The Spanish-speakers generally do not quite fit into that category, as they often have a local connection, and it is also common for a tenant to have a wife and kids either in town or on their way there.

I am known as #6 during my first stay at the Lerman.

Getting to know one another

The way three of the main characters meet is probably the most telling of how the practical organization among these people is conducted. The relationship Zack (see — "Zack", p. 192), Art (see — "Art", p. 200) and John (see — "John", p. 188) have is rather interesting.

The four us of have our first common meeting on the morning of the Sunday after John, Angel and I have helped Zack clean his house (see — "John socializing", p. 99), after which Zack goes to Mexico (see — "Zack physical", p. 84). Zack has just left to go to church with Angel when John appears and asks me which church I am going to go to. I tell him that I have agreed to go to church with Zack, and so he decides to come along. After getting some coffee, we walk over to the church, and sure enough, Zack is waiting outside.

The church is the local chapter of some evangelical denomination and so their singing consists of a mix of pop and gospel. Most of the attendees are Anglo, and the main theme of the sermon that day is that the first tenth of what one earns does not belong to the earner but instead belongs to God (which for them means that one should give it to the church), according to the Bible. After the sermon, the pastor begins healing people. As an example that the healing is "real," he chooses his wife. She sits on the first row and he asks her to come up and tell her story. Before joining him at the altar, she makes sure that she put away her glasses, and once she is standing beside him, she tells the congregation a heart-breaking story of how she has always wanted to be able to see without glasses and how the Lord had made her wish come true one day. When she is finished with her story, the healing begins and several people step up to the altar. The pastor touches their heads one after another they each fall down. Zack is one of those getting healed that day.

As 'public space' the church is clearly segregated between the minority group (Hispanics) and the Anglos. And it is not the Anglos who can bridge the gap, but rather the minority individual Zack who is able to, mainly because he is bi-lingual.

After the church service has ended, we are about to go home when I meet Art at the exit. He asks me whether I care for something to eat, and John immediately joins in, saying that he really "could eat something right now." This is how Art and John meet for the first time, and for a while they hang around each other quite a lot, even though they have completely different interests.

Art leads the way, and none of us spend another second thinking about Zack, who had been standing at the altar when the service ended. During the conversation that night (see — "The Confession", p. 86), Zack shows his disappointment that we had left him behind: "And me, did any of you think about whether I was hungry?"

As the example shows, in some situations, the ethnic group affiliation takes precedence. While John and Art hardly have anything to talk about, they do not realize that yet. But because they both feel certain that the other is equally restrained through his knowledge of the language, they see it as a natural thing to trust one another. On the other hand, John was interested in joining the church service precisely because he had heard that Zack would be there as well.

Art leads us to the Presbyterian Church. Their service has already ended, but they have a monthly potlatch in a meeting room. Art knows some people there and introduces me as "Johann, sociologist from Sweden" and they ask him how his telescope class plans are coming along. Art explains it to me later that day: he has started going to the churches because he thinks several people attending the services are likely to join his telescope class. "But we need some kind of translation; three of those who are interested don't speak any English," Art adds.

At the meeting, the three of us consume as much food we can, while the congregation is approving last year's financial report and electing new leadership.

Although John and I already know Art when he still lives in his car, he does not become part of our little food exchange network at the Lerman until he moves in. This is probably because he is regarded as an unsafe element as long as he lives in his car. When he moves in, I cut a deal with him so whenever I am to pay for some of the ingredients, he uses his food stamp card, and I give him the money. In that way he obtains some money for gas.

Social Life

Sharing

At the Lerman, the Douglasite Hispanic residents Angel, Zack, Blue (#4, a man who never talks much, and sits in the lobby of the Grand as well as the library reading about Hollywood stars from the 1930's), John, and I quickly get together every day to arrange meal preparation. Mr. Fernandez takes me to Wal-Mart one day and takes me by the electric skillets so often while repeatedly pointing out their low prices, that I end up buying one for 20 USD. Angel has a coffee machine, John has food from St. Vincent De Paul's, and Zack always has cans of cheap Food City cola. At first, the economic necessity drives us into preparing the food together as a group

— or at least, that is the excuse we use ourselves for socializing. We put the food out on a table next to the TV area while eating. But it soon extends beyond that. The first few times, we make food with chicken, and the second time we vastly overestimate the quantity of ingredients that we need. So when Blue comes by, John immediately offers some of the food to him. A few days later, as I am sitting in front of the TV, Blue comes walking by. He offers me a Food City Cola. I ask him whether he wants anything in return, but he refuses: "No, no..." A minute later he says, "Well, you can give me an apple one of these days." But when I get up immediately to find an apple in my room, he refuses: "Not now, just one of these days." I never get a chance to give it to him before the following January, about a year later, and he never mentions it again.

We also begin storing food away for Zack when he is at work during mealtime, and we then heat it up when he comes home.

When I return to the Lerman during my second stay, Blue and Mr. Fernandez are the only two residents still there that I had interactions with previously. Most of the newcomers only speak Spanish, and although Blue speaks Spanish perfectly, he is happy that I have returned: "You know, there is old Jose in #9, and we have Mr. Fernandez, and now you came back. I think we're a pretty good crew."

Sex life

Although most residents of the Lerman are men without girlfriends, there are three women around as well.

Prostitution is illegal in the U.S., but there is a woman between 40 and 60 years of age who offers services at the Lerman. Her prices are 5 and 10 USD for two different versions of early morning sex, which she provides around 5am — every morning, walking around knocking on various doors in the motel. Sometimes, she comes back later on in the day, at which time she does not offer any services but instead just walks around the lobby. I do not know how she determines which doors it is wise to knock on, but she never knocks on my door, or perhaps I just never wake up when she does.

She is the sort of prostitute who falls easily into the category of what Anderson called the typical hobo-prostitute: not among the most attractive women, and she also seems to be in a rather unstable situation in life (Anderson 1923, 142–144). On top of that, according to John, she is not very clean, and probably a carrier of sexually transmitted diseases (see — "The prostitute", p. 82).

The night after Zack's afternoon in Mexico (see — "The Confession", p. 86), he tells me that the girl who Mr. Fernandez had introduced as his daughter-in law really is only his ex-daughter-in-law and that she has "the hots" for Zack. I notice it earlier that day, when they are both sitting on the couch. And according to Zack, Blue does not notice what is going on, as he repeatedly goes back and forth between his room and the communal refrigerator, not giving them any time alone at all. When Zack tells me for the first time that the prostitute is offering her services and that Mr. Fernandez daughter-in-law had asked him whether he had been using her services, he replied to her "Why would I be doing her if I could have you in there?" Then for a while they have a casual sexual relationship.

A third woman, appearing to be in her late twenties, comes to the Lerman first as an old acquaintance of Zack's in January. Zack wants nothing to do with her, so he throws her bags, which she had placed inside his room when the door was unlocked, out into the hallway. And then in June she comes back as the sexual partner of a young and fairly attractive man in #6. During this time, both of them are usually lying half naked on the bed with the door open due to the heat, and they rarely talk with others.

What is interesting is the dynamics of the gossip surrounding these three women. While everyone present in the Lerman at the time gossips about all three women, the content differ dramatically. The prostitute is talked about openly, and the fact that she knocks on doors is seen as a curiosity. However, it is not common for anyone to admit to using her services, and there is also very little speculation about whom has used her services. People seem much more interested in whether Zack had managed to "get Mr. Fernandez' daughter-in-law into bed already." The third woman, although equally attractive, is mostly seen as a liability to Zack's trustworthiness; since she is an uncertain character, which serves as proof that Zack had a shady past.

Anderson describes two relationships that the hobo usually has to the women with whom he associates: on one hand there is the woman, often an attractive girl, employed at the mission, and then there is the prostitute. While the former receives a lot of respect, the latter is seen as nothing special (Anderson 1923, 142-144). The way Mr. Fernandez' daughter-in-law is seen is very much in line with this view, and the Lerman residents believe that Mr. Fernandez employs her as well, since is seen mopping the floor every now and then. The fact that the usage of the prostitute's services is of no interest also easily falls in line with her having much lower status.

The third woman falls somewhat outside these categories. She knows both Spanish and English and is seen as manipulative and as a generally shady character. Women like that are dangerous, and Zack's involvement with her shows how he cannot control them. John shows his understanding of this category of women most clearly when I am invited by Lisa and January for dinner one night, and he assumed without having seen them that I had met girls from that category only. John hears a rumor that they have invited me the library a few days in advance of the dinner, and during breakfast he warns me before Art arrives:

> Well, I wouldn't do that [attend the dinner] [...] now, if one of them is a minor, that's jail-bait right there. [...] They're gonna rip off your pants and before you know it, they're crying and everything with the sheriff there and parents and all; you raped them! And you're going right back to jail. And when you get out, you gotta pay for that kid, man! I'm telling you, don't go there!

While the warning about going to jail seems to refer only to the danger of getting accused by minors, the fear of having to pay alimony and the perceived danger of rape by a woman seems real enough, as Blue's statements also confirm when he sees me that night, as he has heard from Mr. Fernandez that I will be going to a different part of town.

The "not so socials"

But there are also those who do not quite fit into the pattern. In room #12 there is an old Hispanic gentleman who I have only seen talk at the senior citizen meetings in the nearby park every Tuesday and Thursday, and there he only speaks Spanish. He is not integrated into the group at the Lerman at all and then one night, when nobody else is in the lobby, he approaches me and says in completely accent-free English: "Hi, my name is Edwin. If the phone rings and they ask for me, you know my name. [...] I don't tell any of the others; they are too nosy." After that conversation I never again hear him speak in English. He turns up at the senior citizen meeting sometimes. He explains in Spanish that he does not want to stop working, as other Hispanics who do tend to fall apart physically.

Another anti-social character is #3 — "Mr. Pipe." I observe him walking around Douglas with his pipe and without saying much. One afternoon John and I meet a man from LA who tells me he is Mr. Pipe's friend at St. Lukes[1]. He tries to sell us his bike, and asks us how his friend is doing. I tell him that I do not know, since he never speaks, and we do not buy the bike. That night at the Lerman, when #3 comes in, he walks right up to me and we have the following exchange:

#3: I heard you have been telling lies about me all over town. Look man, I don't know you and I don't want to know you, is that clear?
JOHANNES: I didn't say anything...
#3: [*seriously aggravated*] Quit lying, I know what you said!
JOHANNES: [*realized the seriousness of the situation*] Yes, sir.
#3: Now you stop talking about me!
JOHANNES: Yes, sir.
#3: And quit calling me 'sir.'
JOHANNES: Yes.

When Mr. Fernandez hears the story, he begins enforcing the rent payments more strictly on tenants who have been delinquent,

---

[1]St. Lukes is a Catholic welfare organization that serves a dinner once a month

Picture 6: Inside the El Espejo kitchen

since Mr. Pipe is one of those who have, and when he talks to John the same way he talked to me a few nights later, Mr. Fernandez does not say anything, but #3 is evicted from the Lerman and is gone a few days later. He also gets ejected from the library a few months later for screaming at the staff, and according to the librarian's son Bruce; he has already been kicked out of a Veterans club he had been a member of.[2]

Chatting at El Espejo

The two people running the juice bar El Espejo, the former 'coyote' Todd who still has to pay off his fine, and the owner and part-time

---

[2]A few weeks later, I observe how Mr. Pipe tries to convince Adolphy (a youngster in his twenties who has gotten a hold of some temporary stipend to work at the library and not to be confused with the Cyber teen Adolphy) that he can sell the old bottles he has found in the trash in order to pay for college for one of his kids. At that time, John believes he has seen him move into one a container behind the Lerman.

journalist Kevin, are both quite poor, but in contrast to the Lerman residents, they are highly educated. They present this to me as their willful decision to stay in Douglas to escape corporate America, even if that means they have to live in poverty.

El Espejo has several different functions. Financially, this is to support Kevin and his family and to help Todd survive until he is free to leave the country again. Socially, it functions as a meeting place for people who like to talk about local, national and global politics from a left-wing government-critical perspective, as well as some other non-political subjects.

The day at El Espejo usually begins when Todd or Kevin, or both, have finished with their morning errands, such as chatting and drinking coffee at the bakery La Gardin. One of the main activities is to read the Arizona Daily Star[3] and when necessary, to fill the refrigerator with fruits from Food City. Kevin also spends some of his time in the El Espejo parking lot fixing the Volvos he has collected, and Todd spends some time reading books, mainly on U.S. foreign policy.

Tom, Bruce's father, comes by El Espejo occasionally. Kevin wonders about Tom's need for social interaction, since he usually stays away for several days and then suddenly shows up again to chat. Edwin Ludszeweit, a retired expert on chicken genetics, comes more frequently, to catch up on what is new around Douglas. And Bridget comes by for hours at a time in order to have Todd help her with her claims against her former husband.

Both Todd and Kevin are fluent in Spanish, and they share a particular affection for the Spanish-speaking countries of the Americas. Todd speaks Spanish whenever he can get away with it, especially when he is somewhat certain that a customer speaks Spanish. Kevin is even annoyed by Hispanics who have stopped speaking Spanish. In a discussion about language politics at schools, he supports a position of forcing Douglas high school students to take Spanish as a subject in school — "else most of these kids would never learn Spanish," he argues.

Nevertheless, nearly all of the people who come to El Espejo to talk extensively with Todd and Kevin do not speak Spanish at

---

[3]The Daily Star is the newspaper of Tucson, Arizona.

all. Unless Kevin's Mexican wife is standing behind the counter, El Espejo is therefore mainly an English-speaking area. But while the question of English and Spanish at El Espejo is primarily an issue of practicality, it is a political issue as well. Not knowing Spanish is permissible for some, in Todd's view, especially if they are not from the area, but generally Todd sees it as a sign of ignorance.

Checking out girls at the library

At the library, there are always quite a number of teen-age girls and boys hanging out — most of whom never really look at books. Besides chitchatting, they make use of the Internet computers that are available. A group of teen-age boys is called the 'Cyber teens' and they are responsible for running the computers. Chris, one of the librarians, is assigned to oversee them, and since he is also a higher-ranking scout, he convinces nearly all of them to also join the scouts. They make up most of the scouts in Douglas and I go on a weekend camp-out with them once.

I ask Adolphy and some of his friends, who are part of the teen-age library crowd, why they choose to hang out there. "To meet chicks," is the very clear answer I get. But it is not only they who are there to meet girls. Art met his wife at a library, and Jerry, a gentleman originally from Maine, who sits in the library just about every day reading the Bible in a little wooden booth, meets a one-armed woman in the library while I am there.

Initially, she is supposed to help Art get started with his telescope business, but when that does not happen, she only spends time with Jerry. At first they just talk, but then he helps her conduct a yard sale, and they sit at the library together creating the sign they want to put up. They end up going on a trip to California, where Jerry never went before, and when they come back, they have broken up. For several weeks she does not come by the library at all, and when she finally does, it is clear that they need to heal some wounds before continuing their relationship. "Hi," she says to Jerry one day, while Art and I are watching from a distance, and then she squeezes herself into the booth that Jerry is sitting in. Jerry tells me his version of the story on July 4th just before the fireworks begin. According to his story, she already has a husband, but since the marriage is registered in Mexico, she thinks that they can just marry again in California — with both marriages continuing. Jerry does not like the idea of being a co-husband, so he chooses not to get married at all.

It is not before I get back to Douglas the second time that I figure out that the lady's second husband is Angel from the Lerman (see p. 191). The fact that Angel is staying in close proximity to the library does not seem to matter; as long as she is inside the English-speaking library, she seems to be sure that she will not directly run into him.

Another clique at the library is a group of retired teachers. One of them had been a headmaster, they are mostly Anglo, and they go to the library every day to read the paper for free and to talk about current events. Art joins their group after a while and also Edwin Ludszeweit comes and visits with this group on a frequent basis. Mostly, the members of the group are conservative — they long for harder punishments of kids in school, they frequently talk about how city people do not understand that wild animals need to be shot rather than preserved, and they speak in favor of more heavily protecting the border to keep illegal immigrants out.

On the other hand, they constantly make jokes about the Christians in town. They call Jerry the "Bible thumper," and churches are described as being "scattered all over town" in addition to those on the church square. As one of them says: "You know if you do read too much of them old books, you get screwed up in your brain." When Edwin talks to them, he seems to accept their premise of immigration being unfavorable, but he also adds: "We have lost that battle already." All the teachers hold the view that President Bush should not be re-elected, and when they hear that the mayor of London, England has called him the most dangerous man around, they all agree that he "sure is right about that one."

While Art spends most of his time at the library reading books, John spends about an hour a day on the Internet and reads the newspaper for another half hour or so, but he never socializes with the group of old teachers. Zack never comes by at all and neither does Angel.

Todd has a fine of a few dollars on his library card, so he never borrows books in his own name and seldom stays at the library long enough for Chris or other members of the staff to talk to him. However, he is there long enough to find interesting new books. Once he asks me to check out a book for him that he has hidden on another shelf inside the library, and according to Bruce, usually it is the head librarian Sarah who lets Todd borrow books on her own card.

The Douglas Cultural Elite

The third place I stay at is the home of Sarah's family, which has a somewhat stronger connection to Todd and Kevin. For example, when rumors spread about 9-11, Kevin went to visit them, because he knew they owned a satellite dish.

The members of the Douglas cultural elite read a lot, and they read collectively. Books are ordered from the library, and the library has a policy of ordering based on the requests of the library patrons. But the privilege to do this is not used very consistently by all members of society. Shortly after I have moved to Todd's house, I once walk down the road toward El Espejo with Bruce as Bicycle Peter, an old Anglo man who has been living in the area for quite a while, rides by on his bike. He stops and hands Bruce a book that he had fastened to the back of his bike. One person requests the book, so the library has purchased it, and then that same person checks it out. After that, the book is passed around and is read by all, or at least nearly all, of the entire cultural elite group. And it is by no means the only book that makes the round either. One book after another makes the round and is read by essentially the same group of people. Bruce, Todd, Kevin, Tom, Bicycle Peter, and Edwin Ludszeweit all use the influence they have over Sarah and the library, to order the books they are interested in. For a while I am also part of the loop. Not all members read all the books and some, like Todd, read a lot more; nevertheless it creates a circle of people who all have a similar knowledge horizon. Once I start calling them the "Douglas Cultural Elite," and the name sticks, especially with Bruce and Todd. "We should make t-shirts and hand them out to the Cyber teens," Bruce jokes once.

The books they read are to a large extent critical of President Bush and the U.S. government, and Sarah finds herself in a dilemma, wanting to be politically neutral and at the same time having no respect for pro-Bush authors such as Ann Coulter or Michael Savage. She talks at length about how a right-winger has had sent her a letter complaining about the selection of books they have at the Douglas library, even though she already had purchased several of "their books." At the same time, her son Bruce criticizes her for even having the Michael Savage book at all. Sarah answers the letter by suggesting the right-wing books that the library already has, instead of ordering more right wing literature. In contrast, when I go up to the counter to ask whether they can get *The Condor Years* (a book about Pinochet's transcontinental terror network that I view as being a rather special interest book) from the library in Sierra Vista which already has the book, the librarian Bill, who is sitting behind the counter, tells me: "No, we cannot get their copy, they have restrictions on interlibrary loans, but we can order it." About ten days later I receive a personal e-mail from Maria stating that the book is available at the library, waiting to be picked up.

The Lerman residents gone bookish

Anderson really goes out of his way to describe the extensive reading that hobos engage in. According to Anderson, hobos are generally inclined to read both daily papers and radical literature on utopias that are to come and which will provide the hobos with a better life. (Anderson 1923, 185) To a certain extent, this is also true of the Lerman crowd; all the English-speaking men except Zack go to the library on a daily basis to study the Douglas Dispatch, and sometimes they also peruse the Arizona Daily Star or the Arizona Republic. However, the amount of progressive literature that they read is limited.

Of those staying at the Lerman, only Art extensively reads progressive literature, but John, to the best of my knowledge, only reads the Bible and a book on King Arthur. One of Art's favorite writers is Adam Smith, and the way Art interpret his work, today's American society is very far from the ideal society as Adam Smith portrayed it. Art believes that we need to eliminate monopolies in order for true capitalism to flourish.

But Art's thinking is not strictly limited to the ideas of Adam Smith. During my reading of *The Capital*, Art is the primary person I discussed it with, as he tries to argue some of the more complicated aspects of the value-theory. Since a lot of *The Capital* was written precisely as argument against Smith and his contemporaries, the debates with Art on the subject are extremely enlightening.

What is interesting is that none of the Lerman residents, and others who have a lifestyle similar to Jerry, Stan or Bicycle Peter, are as interested in day-to-day national politics as the Douglas Cultural Elite is, or in voting at national elections, since they look instead at the longer term and issues on a fundamentally theoretical base (Biblical morals to some, and theoretical works like Adam Smith to others). At the same time, they are very interested in local news and rumors, although they usually are the last to know breaking local news that involve people beyond the Lerman or St. Vincent de Paul, due to their relatively small contact network.

Ghetto people at La Gardin

La Gardin, the bakery in front of Todd's house, was only established a few months before I arrive. A family that has another bakery across the border and also one in Tucson runs it, but they seem to spend most of their time in Douglas. The father had been an illegal immigrant and claims to have seen the KKK when trying to cross 11 years ago. Later, he had severely injured his leg while working for an American company, so it had to be amputated and so during my time in Douglas he is walking on a wooden leg. He claims that he had received a settlement, which allowed him to buy the bakeries. "It's his American dream coming true," one of the boys from the bakery translates for him as he speaks to me about his current situation.[4]

Two girls, Michelle and Lori stand mainly behind the counter. Michelle had a little daughter who runs around the bakery and only speaks Spanish, and Lori has just begun her studies at Cochise College. In the back room are the father and mother, as well as two young men in their twenties or thirties, and 19 year old Francisca, a daughter of the owner from outside the marriage. The young men drive around in their car a good portion of the day, and after I have moved in with Todd and they hear about me, they scream "whazup Killer Todd?" whenever they see me walking down the street, or when I enter Todd's house while they are in the bakery, or in the parking lot. I hear them yell this in both Agua Prieta and all over Douglas, although they seem to concentrate on 10th street in Douglas, where they also are involved in quite a bit of cruising, driving down the street 5 or 6 times a night. When I ask them why they say that, it becomes clear that they think I am Todd's son, and if not, then I must be part of his family in some other way. "And you look all 'killer' " they explain about the rest of the expression. "You got some chicks around town as well?" they ask, and although I clearly do not, I encourage them by moving my eyelids up and down a single time. "Whew!" they comment, "He is Pimp Todd as well."

John's first meeting with La Gardin is through the Douglas Dispatch. He had walked by La Gardin a couple of times, but one morning there is a presentation of the La Gardin staff in the Dispatch. "It's our bakery!" John exclaims somewhat excitedly when he sees it. Bruce ridicules the statement sometime later: "It's all ours; everything in the newspaper is somehow ours here in Douglas," when I tell him about John's reaction. After John finishes reading the article, he asks me to come with him to eat there. By that time, I have already been there once with the Barkers, but when I go there with John, it is quite a different experience.

---

[4]A few months after I leave the second time, I hear about the bakery being busted for smugling Mexicans and Mexicans across the border. However, according to Bruce and Edwin, most of the evidence is lost during a failed 'fax attempt' when the Douglas police tries to send their findings to Tucson. The bakery can therefore open the next day as if nothing has happened. It is unclear to both Bruce and me why they could not attempt at faxing the evidence a second time.

The first time we go there together, John checks all the prices quite carefully and then decides to buy a burrito. Lori, who was introduced to me by the Barkers the last time I was there, is selling, and seems to react to the fact that I now seem to be part of a quite different social layer. At first she does not say anything, as we give our orders. John gives his long and confusing order for a burrito, "not too soft and with some chorizo, but also not too much...." I just ask for a standard burrito from their menu. When our burritos arrive, he starts complaining that the meat is raw and has it sent it back to the kitchen. But then he does not want any meat at all and orders a completely different burrito.

As soon as we are finished, Lori asks me if I had been there before, and she waits until the next time I come, alone, to ask who John is. John feels that the staff is against him, and so he does not come back there any more for several months, until we finally go there again together upon my suggestion.

When we finally come back to La Gardin, he suggests that his burrito had taken so long to prepare because it had been shipped all the way from his family in Arkansas in order to poison him. That is the absolute last time he comes there with me.

In the months before I arrive, there had been an institution called the 'Wednesday Morning Coffee' at La Gardin, which included Todd, Kevin, Tom, Edwin, Bruce and Bicycle Peter. No further meetings are held during my time there, but it has built a social structure among the characters involved which lasts beyond the meetings — and which turns into the Douglas Cultural Elite.

And still, the Barkers and Todd go there quite a bit. During my time at Todd's, we often both come there two or more times a day, especially during week end mornings, when the Barkers also show up independently and we eat with all of them. After I have moved out of Todd's house, I sometimes meet him there in the morning well before the Barkers get up, and then I go back there once the Barkers come by.

The entire time at La Gardin, an Agua Prieta radio station broadcasting Mexican music is played over speakers, which seem to be inadequate for the chosen volume level. Although the owner makes an investment in new cupboards that look quite expensive, the speakers are not being exchanged for better ones. At the same time as the cupboards is being upgraded, the English menu disappears and from then on one has to read Spanish. After this, Tom states with a somewhat bitter voice one morning: "It is getting very Mexican in here." La Gardin gets very full and everyone except Tom, Bruce and I speak Spanish there.

None of the others from the Lerman ever come there, and neither does anybody else from the library other than Sarah and Bicycle Peter, except during the "Arts in the Park," an annual event in 10th street park sponsored by the library, when several of the library staff members go there because it is so close by.

When I return to Douglas, Kevin, Tom and Roger have started meeting at the Starbucks instead. "It got too Mexican there," is the explanation I get, "the food wasn't all that good and the music just got louder and louder."

Games at 10th Street Park

10th Street Park is only the size of one regular block and only a block away from the library. In the middle of it the city has a small house, which contains two pool games, a table soccer game, and a few other games that are seldom in use. There is also a sink, and under it, there is a plastic box which contains all the items that are needed for the senior citizen meeting which is held on Tuesday and Thursday mornings: cookies, tea bags, coffee and the sign up sheet. In the afternoons, the place is open so that the youngsters have access to the games. One person from the recreational department is assigned to the Center, although almost no senior citizen ever seems to show up. During the first week, it is Monica, an ex-employee of Sarah, who runs the place.

I know the place is going to be open, but I do not quite know when, so I sit outside at 8am one morning in January waiting for the senior citizens to come by. Juan, the park gardener, is the only one to show up, but he invites me inside to drink some coffee. He takes his time with the cleaning and the prison has also given him a helper in the form of a convict who has been jailed "I think for bank robbery," as Juan guesses. Juan had been in Germany while he was in the ARMY, but he came back to Douglas when his tour of duty was complete. He seems to know Monica well, and after a while he leaves us alone. No senior citizen ever shows up and so I talk to Monica until it is time to close. She is in her early thirties and has already had three children, and she has been married for 14 years. She is from across the border, while her Anglo husband is from Douglas. She talks a lot about her husband's father, with whom she has much in common. She also makes sure that on the following Thursday he will show up.

That Thursday I meet Monica once more, and it happens to be the last time before she quits. Instead Arlie starts showing up. Arlie hates the place more than anything, as "there is nothing to do." During the first week, again not a single senior citizen shows up. Arlie is my age, and she is looking forward to go to college, but she does not want to leave quite yet. She tells me that her father offered to pay for everything she wanted, but according to her she "preferred to go work." she does not explain why. Her ultimate dream is to go a technical college, away from Douglas. Most conversations are held in English at the senior citizens meeting, but when Monica shows up during the meeting, she talks with Arlie in Spanish. According to Arlie, they "always do that."

I do not go to the senior citizen meeting often as it becomes more and more clear that there are never any senior citizens showing up. During John's first two weeks in town, when he is completely out of money while waiting for his next government check, I send him there, so he will be able to get something to eat, if only the cookies they give out for free. He tells me later about how he beat Arlie in playing pool. After that, he also asks me several times whether I want to go there with him, and a few times we end up going together. John would prefer to show up without a shirt, but I tell him that I would like for both of us to wear shirts, so instead he goes with his shirt unbuttoned all the way. He starts talking to Arlie, but to his disappointment, she hardly ever looks up but instead is busy playing games on her cell phone while John and I usually play a game of pool in which he smashes me completely, before we go on to Mexico, El Espejo or the library.

I do not go there very much when it is open for the teenagers, but Luis, one of the Cyber teens, knows one of the girls quite well who are responsible for opening the Center, and he arranges for us to talk to each other over a cell phone which may or may not have been his. He thinks that I should try to get together with her, as she is "way better than all the other girls," as he explains. She is one of the few Anglo youngsters in Douglas. All of the Cyber teens seem familiar with the meeting place, but they have all chosen to stay mainly around the library instead.

At the same park, there are also two stands of fast food most of the time. On one side there is a hot dog stand and on the other there is a taco stand. John and the Barkers are frequent patrons of both stands, and also Maria and her friends come to the hot dog stand at night when cruising. Monica first tells me about the taco stand and that it is the best taco stand around. She used to go there every single day, while she worked at the library.

Living history at the Douglas Wendt house

The Douglas historical society is a group that mainly consists of older Anglos hanging around the Douglas Wendt house. The three main characters I meet there are Denise Hansen, who had been working at the Dispatch until recently, a woman whose ancestors came from Sweden and whose daughter is one of the teachers at the high school and whose grandchild hangs around the library, and Lou, one of the few who openly admit being Republican. During some of the time, Oscar is also using the back room in order to do research for a student council president reunion, which never actually happens.

The first time I enter the Douglas Wendt house I am with Oscar, and he has not been there since high school several years earlier. He greets Lou with: "Remember me?" Lou does not, and he does not remember me either when I come back a few weeks later. Nevertheless, when he sees me at Food City in June, another few months later, he asks me when I will come by again. Lou sees himself as belonging to an opposition to those in power in Douglas. His main focus is that "they," meaning the elite around the mayor to which he does not belong, do not know how to run the city properly, are afraid of changing the population pattern, and are corrupt to the core. As an example of how bad the decisions that the city council makes are, he shows us a model of a bridge that is on display in the Douglas Wendt house. The real bridge had been at the intersection of the train tracks and Highway 80, the road going to Bisbee from Douglas. The city council voted to remove it a few years earlier, since the train had stopped operating. "Other cities build these things just to attract visitors," Lou explains. Another problem is the economic policy the city is pursuing. "How do you get business to town?" Lou asks and he seems to expect an answer for a few seconds, "you build golf courses of course!" According to Lou, it is a proven economic policy that the number of visitors increases in proportion to the increase in available golf courses. I try to argue that there is already one golf course, but Lou thinks that it is obvious that one is just not enough.

As an example of the level of corruption, he tells us that the police have a list of "untouchables," that the police cannot lay a hand on under any circumstances.

Although Oscar and Lou do not know much about one another to start out with, Lou makes sure to frequently include Oscar in the conversation, in an attempt to show that they are both part of the same opposition to the mayor and his clique. Oscar picks it up and shows small gestures to indicate that he agrees, such as smiles and small laughs timed during the pauses between sentences as Lou is speaking. When we have left Lou and the Douglas Wendt house behind, I question the plan for economic progress that Lou had proposed. Oscar partially agrees, "but he is right about the corruption and the incompetence of the city council," he comments.

When I come back the last time, Lou tells me that he feels that all the intermixing between Anglos and Mexicans recently is just part of the general process of degradation of society. He then goes on to say that his own grandson is half Mexican, and he quickly qualifies his earlier statement by saying that his heritage that goes back to the revolutionary war will not disappear completely, but that it will be weakened.

None of the people from any of the places mentioned above visit the Douglas Historical Society during my time there, except Oscar, who is there quite a bit, and Denise, who visits the library occasionally. Todd calls it 'The Douglas Hysterical Society' but it is just a place that is largely ignored, since there is nothing controversial about it — it is just a very U.S. American place. Todd originally had gotten to know Denise when she employed him at the newspaper, and Sarah also knows her quite well from her time employed the library.

Fascists at the gun shop

Oscar is also the first one to go to the gun shop with me. He is a member of the NRA, although he does not own a gun, he thinks that it will be helpful to be pro-NRA when he runs for President (see — "Oscar, first Hispanic president", p. 95).

In addition to the two shopkeepers, Bob Waczkovic and Garst Williams, I notice English-speaking Anglo men between the ages of thirty and sixty coming and going all day, although it seems that they come more to talk and rarely to buy anything. Except for Oscar, none of them ever show up at any of the other hangouts. And just about everyone from the other places avoids the gun shop clique. Todd calls them 'the fascists,' and Bruce just mocks their window display showing disgust when he takes me home one night to the Lerman.

Both of the shopkeepers seem aware of how others feel about them, and when I ask them why they dare put up a sign promoting a Republican in a largely Democratic town, Bob tells me that the Democratic party and the mafia are essentially the same thing and it is only his weapons that give him confidence that nothing is going to happen as a result of the pro-Republican poster.

The two of them do not characterize themselves as fascists, and it is a label mainly Todd applies to them. Although not everyone would go to that extreme, they are definitely right-wingers and are known throughout town for their right-wing opinions (see — "U.S. American Nationalist", p. 156).

Cross-spatial events

John's good-bye reception

Shortly before John flies off to New York (see — "Leaving Town", p. 191), Art and I have a good-bye reception for him in the parking lot behind the library, and I design a poster for the event. On the morning of the event, I go around Douglas to get all the people who know John to sign his good-bye poster and then I tape it to the stand. Art sits on a bench on the sidewalk next to the parking lot with soft drinks. It is all planned to start at 11am, so I go over to John at 10:45 to make sure he will come. But for the first time I have ever observed, John has a friend visiting. John says he has been together in prison with him for 4.5 years. He had seen him at the post office and the man recognized his voice. John offers me some coffee and the man tells me about how he has broken up with his wife. After giving John the advice to come back to Douglas soon (see also p. 164) he goes on to address both of us. He tells us that he has some "weed" in his pocket that he offers to smoke with us. I decline, but I do not think fast enough to realize that John's assurances about going to the library "very soon" (I tell him Art has something important to tell him) will inevitably be broken with his ex-prison-mate around. The ceremony starts as planned at 11:00am and I am sitting out there with only Art for some minutes until I go into the library and get Adolphy to come out there with us. Art immediately starts telling him about airplane diesel engines, so he leaves quickly to get his friend Marcos (who lives in the same apartment complex as John). After another few minutes Art intercepts Stan as he is entering library and convinces him to join us. Stan likes to listen to his wild ideas. I then leave to get John once more.

The time is 11:15 when I meet the two boys Adolphy and Marcos on the way, so we all go to John's room together. When we arrive, John's door is locked and he does not answer, so we head over to his church in order to find out whether the pastor, Carlos, had any information about John. He does not, so we go back to the reception area and they hang around for a while. At 11:45, I decide to go over to John's place again and this time the door is open. The friend is still in there and they have each been drinking a large bottle of beer and start to offer me some while they are putting their clothing back on. I decline and start getting more aggressive, insisting that John has to come to the library immediately. John's friend then leaves and John puts his beer in a paper cup with the words "this beer needs to go for a walk" and walks over to the library with me. John starts crying a little while walking, and combined with that fact that he is getting dressed when I go there, I get the hint that they have been having sex together while the door was locked. John is very Bible-read and strongly homophobic, so he probably has some guilt complex about it. As John says himself, in jail "one needs to get along with everybody," and as it seems that includes having sex with other members of one's sex as well.

Halfway there, John throws his beer in the bushes. He is very drunk. He admits having smoked the "weed" with his prison friend. When we arrive at the library and John sees the table with cookies and Art sitting besides it he asks: "Oh, you're doing a fund-raiser, huh?" I ask him whether he recognizes the picture on the poster, and his ability to speak suddenly vanishes; the last thing he says is "and all my friends signed it!" Stan asks him whether he is going to New York City or to somewhere else in the state of New York and he either does not get the question or just cannot answer anything. I roll the poster up for him so he can take it home and then he stands there for about 15 minutes sipping on a Squirt, unrolling the poster every couple of minutes to focus on another detail of it. At the same time, he is constantly about to cry, but I have a suspicion that it is not just about this event. When he finally goes inside the library, he shows the poster to the librarians and as he is leaving the library, he tells Sarah that he is probably going to be back in Douglas in September, when it gets cold in New York.

The event is talked about a lot, and although the older Anglos do not quite understand what the purpose of it all had been, all the teenagers seem to agree that he had needed a proper farewell reception.

The drug war

On a weekend near Easter time, there is a border horse race. "It's the mayor's great pride," Sarah says. The event is held west of Douglas along the borderline, with Mexican and American horses competing against one another. I go there, but since I do not see much of interest, I ride my bike back home, to avoid getting sunburned.

A few days later, there is news around town that a van with blackened windows had driven up to a restaurant in Agua Prieta and three men had jumped out, then had gone into the restaurant and shot three guests and a waiter with their machine guns before disappearing. All of those who had been shot at were involved with the horses, but also drugs, it is reported.

Many of those hanging around El Espejo want to figure out the exact circumstances. First I hear from Kevin, that Edwin has called and said the story is that a woman from Tucson came to the race and bet 300,000 unofficially on the Mexican side. She had won, but they would not pay her off, so she had gone back to Tucson to hire the hit man.

Later that day, when I ask Edwin about the story while we are riding his pickup, the theory has been already discarded, because she would have had to bet on horses from both the U.S. and Mexico if she was were to win that large an amount.

The next theory I hear is that the Mexican federal police did it, but Todd does not believe in that theory because, as he argues, this theory is solely based on the fact that the cars were black, and the Mexican federal police uses such cars.

"The dust needs to settle a little and then everything will be much clearer in a couple of days," Kevin argues. Within the next few days, another 11 people get shot in Agua Prieta. Kevin finally concludes: "It seems it was drug related; one family got too strong and now the police is thinning them out." Kevin also points out that several of those shot had a warrant for them in the U.S. so that they could not cross the line into the U.S.

Bruce, Tom and Sarah just follow the story without getting much involved with the puzzle surrounding it. It becomes part of Sarah's life, as one of her employees is related to some of those involved in the initial killing. On the day after the initial shootings, Edwin comes by the library and tells Art loudly what has happened according to the current theory. Sarah tells us later: "I was just about to throw Edwin out today when he started talking that loud." One of the girls working at the check out counter that day had an uncle who was killed in the shootings, and Sarah knows about it because the girl asked for time off for the funeral.

It seems that since the Anglos are not as involved with the families who wage various drug wars in Agua Prieta, they nevertheless all care about it and they try to be as close to the source of the information as possible. Kevin even defends it: "People tend to think of Mexico when talking of how brutal it can get and some ask me whether it is safe to go there. And there is violence; that is true. [...] But it is not like in Tucson where someone just does a drive by shooting and kills people who he has no relationship to. Here the shootings are only among those who are involved so you can avoid it if you aren't involved."

Art and John do not hear anything about the shootings until I tell them about it, and in contrast to the local teenagers, John does not think that it requires a moratorium on crossing over to Mexico (see also p. 93).

The election

Another event that is to take place while I am in Douglas is the election for mayor. William Dell shot at one of Todd's dogs (without killing it) as he claims he was attacked, before I come to Douglas, and so Todd is the most negative about him, although he is a Democrat. But also most others I talk to have very low opinions of the mayor. Art views him as the "Mexican candidate" while Alexis Sanders is the "Anglo candidate." Before the elections, I consider interviewing Sanders, but I am not able to conduct the interview until after the elections. When Art and John hear about me going to interview him, they each want to talk to him as well. Art wants to tell him how he could get new jobs to Douglas by investing in a telescope factory, and John just wants to ask for a job. After the elections, Art wants to see him to tell him how he could have won the election, but neither John nor Art ever dare to go to see him.

Sarah is the one who is the quietest about the election, and Bruce and Todd thought that at the next election she should be nominated for mayor, as she is "the most well-known city employee" in Douglas. "You must be out of your mind!" is Sarah's reaction to their proposal repeatedly. Except for Art, there is a common conception that Alexis Sanders "doesn't stand a snowball's chance in hell," but that does not stop those strongly opposed towards William Dell from voting for him.

Oscar tells me that he had interviewed Sanders before the elections, and that Sanders had started sweating during the interview. He liked the fact that the mayor was clearly on the side of the 'illegal immigrants,' although he also sees him as involved in corruption. Denise Hansen explains: "With his father and his brother involved in all that corruption, it just is hard to believe that William has a totally white shirt." Also Edwin talks a lot about the corruption that surrounds the mayor, but rumors have it that Edwin himself had been involved with the mayor and his circle earlier and had just recently broken out of it.

Sanders' campaign strategy is to put some of the Douglas Bulldogs on central street corners with signs supporting him a few days before the election, while Dell hangs around Food City even more than he usually does and is extra friendly with everybody. I wish him good luck and he answers "I appreciate that," before he goes on chitchatting with some of the employees — as he does most days.

On Election Day, John is mistaken for William Dell when we eat at Paddies, and John is one of the few I had met that really support the mayor. "He might just be one of them good old boys," is his reaction when he hears that he might be involved in the ownership of the Lerman, "to give all them poor people a place to stay."

William Dell wins the election by a large margin, which comes as no surprise to most. I am at Douglas Coffee when the Dispatch comes out that day, and the owner sends me over to a gas station to pick it up. It seems to him, as well as the Barkers I find out later, more important that Brissa Gomez lost her district to Dr. Perez. Both like Brissa very much, while they do not know much about

Dr. Perez.[5]

According to the owner of Douglas Coffee, Sanders could not have done much better no matter what he did. "He could have built new schools, but we just got new schools. Or he could bring business to town, but who would come?" he concluded. When I talk to Alexis Sanders, he seems surprised that he did not win. He blames it on the lack of courage in the people of Douglas, who do not dare to revolt against the power structure that is in place. He expects that next time people will form small groups of supporters that will then form pockets of resistance which will overthrow the mayor and his elite.

Conclusion

As we have seen, the various places do not all create a single hegemonic space, although the state is very much present, at least in the background of all of the above events. In the library, the Douglas Wendt house and 10th Street Park it is present in the form of a direct financier, and the state's rules for control of these properties are applied directly. At the Lerman, La Gardin, El Espejo, and the gun shop, it is present mainly as the law, which people then try to circumvent, and such actions are coordinated through meetings at these places.

Nevertheless, even though the U.S. state involves itself to some degree nearly everywhere, the identity that is connected to places in Douglas is only partially U.S. American. And that is really not enough for a country that wants to exert 'hegemonic power;' the main objective is the complete removal of 'bleeding boundaries,' that is, the elimination of any areas in which the hegemonic culture is challenged (Alonso 1994, 384).

Given that Douglas is situated in territory under control of the U.S. government, the hegemonic power of the United States therefore seems fundamentally weak. Maybe as a consequence, the

---

[5]Brissa had been known for trying to persuade bar-owners in Agua Prieta to not let Douglas kids under the age of 16 drink during her term. Somewhat later, it is reported that Dr. Perez voted against the budget and that he told Mr. Dell personally that he will not help carry out his "program of corruption." This is counted as a triumph for the oppositional forces of Douglas.

idea of the nation as an organism of its own is only supported by a segment of the Douglas population I meet.

However, concluding that the U.S. as a hegemonic national identity is weak is not the same as saying that Huntington is correct in his analysis of Hispanics destroying U.S. nationalism. The most important fact here is that the dividing line between groups runs across language barriers, although these necessarily restrict fluid communication: all the Lerman residents are much more closely connected to one another than they are to any of the other groups, despite their internal language differences. And also La Gardin, El Espejo, 10th Street Park and even the library, although to a lesser extent, stand out as places where both English and Spanish is spoken at times, and which at the same time also represent the power of a certain group.

Furthermore, the main places in which resistance towards the current system is being contemplated, El Espejo, the gun shop and some people at the library, it is Anglos who represent this resistance and not Hispanics.

In his analysis, which confines everyone to solidarity with one's own culture, Huntington has forgotten that resistance can also come from within. And while many Hispanics with strong personal ties to Mexico believe in the 'American way of life,' it is the Anglos who are the first ones to break actively out of the hegemonic space once the system fails to provide prosperity for them.

Chapter 2

Money — Structural Networks of Dependency

THE people of Douglas who I am examining have widely varying backgrounds. Mostly this is due to the very transient nature that much of the U.S. has. The different backgrounds also come with different economic situations, as I will try to present here. The economic situations can be divided into two issues: the issue of how much money that each one has coming in every month and how they spend it, and the issue of how each person conceptualizes money.

Regarding access to money and how people acquire it, we should be able to observe differences of class — which will allow us to see how large the production network they are involved in is.

The media mostly distinguishes between a lower or working class, a middle class and an upper class. The problem with that way of classifying is that it's not clear who exactly falls into which category. Most people therefore classify themselves as middle class, and anyone earning significantly less or more is placed in the lower or the upper class. In contrast, the Marxist way of classifying people into classes is based on where their place in the production process is.

Although there are class distinctions in place in Douglas, it is hard, if not impossible, to receive much personal financial information from those earning significantly above the average. It is probably even harder in Douglas compared to many other places, due to the illegal nature of much of the business that they are — allegedly — involved in. Another reason is that the number of people living with extraordinarily high incomes is in all likelihood very small in Douglas[1]. Those earning the average or less than the average income can be distinguished from one another, but only to a certain degree due to the high unemployment rate. It is therefore not so important which class definition we use on distinct individuals in this case, since the classes overlap quite a bit.

Regarding the issue of the informants' belief in money and its value, my aim is to be able to see in which ways my informants define the limits of the exchange networks they are a part of.

In this chapter, I choose to take exchange networks to mean independently working economic entities — a kind of community that is not only based on whom the individuals enjoy being around, but also on the interdependencies between individuals. But how large is such a network of interdependence? And how large do people believe that such a network might be?

To find out about this, it can be helpful to look at how Marx (1999) conceptualizes what he calls 'generalized money' — that is, a commodity that is only used in order to exchange other commodities in a market more easily. His analysis starts out by looking at how goods are exchanged for each other and how in addition to their 'use value,' which is unique for each produced good, they acquire an 'exchange value,' which makes them exchangeable for other goods. First Marx describes how two commodities can be exchanged with each other, but since these again can be exchanged with other commodities, and those again can be exchanged with other commodities, all commodities will ultimately be exchangeable, and the 'exchange value' will be expressed in quantities of one of the commodities, even though this commodity might not even be part of he particular exchange one desires to make. Later on, in order to make things more orderly and for purposes of standardization, the exchangers choose a single such commodity, and everyone considers it no longer as an ordinary commodity, but rather as a

---

[1]Exact figures are not available to anyone because illegal activities are usually kept of the record.

means of exchange as its primary characteristic — and that is what generalized money is. Marx sees the main determining factor for each commodity's exchange value as the amount of labor that went into it, and the 'price,' determined by supply and demand, is seen as revolving around that exchange value. Once generalized money exists, new commodities are immediately compared to it in terms of exchange value, and no one looks at the exact amount of labor that has gone into its production. (Marx 1999, 13–93)

The power of labor to create value is Marx's main point, but it is not what we will concern ourselves further with here. What is important in this case is the social construction of the money commodity. From Marx's description, it is not clear whether he thinks of the creation of money as a historical process, or whether it is a social process that is ongoing and into which children are socialized. In either case, the process of social construction needs to be based on a certain network of exchange that has a geographic form, both because the amount of work that goes into a commodity varies geographically, and because the commodities that are circulated in order to give birth to the concept of money also vary geographically.

This network of exchange might also be seen as the 'community of interdependence' or simply the 'division of labor'. By looking at how people define money, we should therefore be able determine what is a part of the network and what is not.

Let us look at the following descriptions of some prominent informants and to what degree they can give us answers to our questions.

Mr. Fernandez

No one seems to know whether Mr. Fernandez is the owner or just the manager of the Lerman hotel (see — "The pasta crisis — social life at the Lerman ", p. 17). He himself specifies it as his hotel, but in the early days he also works at a construction site in order to "pay the rent," since many rooms are empty right after Christmas. One theory that I hear from several sources is that the mayor owns the hotel, but there is no one who can confirm it. No administrative person other than Mr. Fernandez and his daughter-in-law is ever seen around the Lerman, but a few months into spring, Mr. Fernandez enters an office across from the library on 10th street, every day at various times for several weeks, into which the mayor also goes every now and then and reappears wearing a different set of clothing (see also — "Checking out girls at the library", p. 26). A group of retired teachers, who at the time have their daily meetings at a table inside the library close to the windows facing 10th street, speculates about whether the mayor's brother owns it.

When Mr. Fernandez finds out within the first ten minutes of meeting me that I do not have a car, he retracts his requirement for a key deposit and when I come back a day later with the first batch of my belongings, he tells me that he will help me get set up "with Food Stamps and everything." The first time I think that I probably should not bother explaining to him that I am not eligible, but when I am completely moved in a few days later, he repeats the offer and makes it clear that he really means it. "Just go down there and talk to Mrs. Tapia and say that I sent you and you will get your food stamps," he says while pointing at a building from the back porch of the Lerman. I tell him that I, as a foreigner on a tourist visa, can hardly be eligible, but he continues telling me to go down there and ask for the Food Stamps using his name as reference. I also tell him that I do have enough money, but he keeps on saying that I should go and get both food stamps and food from the food bank. "You can use your money for other things, and if you don't eat it all, you can give me the rest, and I'll take it to the Mexican prisoners across the line," he says. I begin to think that his insistence might have something to do with the amount of food I store in the communal refrigerator. I have heard a claim somewhere that Europeans buy less food at a time but they generally go shopping daily and so they tend to store less food than Americans. So one day I go out and buy larger amounts of everything and put it all in the refrigerator. That night I have the following short conversation with Mr. Fernandez in the lobby:

JOHANNES: Mr. Fernandez, have you seen, I bought groceries today!

MR. FERNANDEZ: Yes, but you should have gotten food stamps!
JOHANNES: But I'm not a U.S. citizen!
MR. FERNANDEZ: So what? Don't you eat?

As we can see, Mr. Fernandez' access to money is related to the state, although in a rather indirect way. His immediate source of money is of course the individual and private tenants, but the ultimate source of his income is from welfare agencies that give or lend money to those staying at the Lerman. However, he seemingly does not consider borders as a barrier to what money can be used for or who can get access to money; it is all a question of whether the agency can be convinced that the eligibility requirements are being met. However, officially, rights are distributed unequally and according to citizenship, and diverting food to Mexican prisoners seems to be an act of trying to even it out.

At first, I believed Mr. Fernandez to hold a community view that goes across the border. But then I notice how he believes that even I — not from anywhere close to the borderland or Mexico — am discriminated against in his view because I do not receive food from the food bank (which I would argue goes beyond what you would give to someone you merely count as a foreign guest). His sense of solidarity originates in a concept of injustice that extends beyond the local and beyond the national.

John

John McConnell has been on a 1000 USD monthly social security check since the 1970's for "not having all [his] noodles together," as he says himself, "but you know, who does these days." Still, he is looking for jobs. John brings a strong mistrust of Afro-Americans from Arkansas. He also expects to be cheated on his utility bills as well as by the landlord, due to his white skin color. At the same time, in Mexico, he can hardly go by any beggar without trying to get him some food from somewhere. Several times when we walk around Agua Prieta and we pass a person or family sitting on the sidewalk, I try to just walk on, while John insists on us stopping to check our pockets for spare change. A few times he goes as far as entering some nearby restaurant to buy a meal that he then

Picture 7: John got a free juice
at El Espejo.

hands out. "Seeing something like that really makes you feel kind of down," he says one time as we walk by an obviously needy man when we both have already spent all our money on food for ourselves.

John presents himself as being very rich, as many others in Douglas do. According to his story, he has been a millionaire since the age of five as a result of a lawsuit. Now, his entire family is out to get his money and they are trying to deprive him of his legal ownership of the family home.

When I first meet John at the Posada Lerman, I am hanging around Zack at the time. All of us are better off than Art, because he has to live in his car. Zack is working as a day laborer on construction, John has his monthly check, and I have money coming from my Danish student stipend. For the first few days though, John is completely broke. He has to wait for his monthly check for two weeks and has absolutely no money other than that. He therefore walks down to St. Vincent de Paul's[2] and gets them to pay for his rent at the Lerman. He also starts helping them out in their

---

[2]St. Vincent de Paul's is a catholic welfare organization.

thrift store and comes home most nights with bags of groceries that they have given him there.

It is during these early days, that Mr. Fernandez, Zack, and John have determined that I need to get money from some place, because I am obviously very poor, as far as they can tell. But because I keep telling them there is absolutely no reason to do so, John decides that he needs to push me into it. One day he asks me whether I could come to St. Vincent de Paul's with him, and while we are there sitting at the table waiting for the food to be served, he stops one of the nuns and tells her: "This guy might want to talk to the bishop." She starts asking him questions, and while I contemplate my escape, John happily tells her everything about me that he knows. When he gets to the story about me carrying a German passport with a tourist visa, her objections tell me that I have to step in. I explain my situation to her with John listening. "Isn't he lucky" she says to John, while she welcomes me to eat there anytime I want. Apparently she was not quite sure whether she should believe my story or whether she was to take it to just be my 'story,' like John had done.

When she is gone John says: "I still think it's unfair that you're not allowed to work or get any help."

After about six weeks, Mr. Fernandez gets a place for John in a regular apartment that his nephew rents out a block away for the same amount per month as his room at the Lerman. John gets a sofa, a coffee maker, a mattress and a few other items, but he remains without a bed frame for his entire stay.

The nephew is also able to arrange for John to work at the Grand to wash dishes, and John lasts at the job for about a week. One of the first days he lends his room key to Art and me so that we can make food and then he asks us to bring the key over to the Grand even though we will still be in his room when he comes back himself. I walk over there, and ask for John as he has instructed me to do. It takes a while for him to come out, as he is back in the kitchen, and I hand him the key quickly. But John wants to talk a little first while the cashier lady watches: "So has everything worked out alright?" And I chat for a little while with him. "He wants them to know that he is hanging around smart people," is Art's analysis, "he wants them to know that he is not just right out of prison."

The work is irregular, and John must check daily whether they will have work for him. One day there is a huge banquet at the Grand, and so they ask John to move some chairs to and from the basement since the elevator operator is not there while he is in the kitchen. John explains afterwards:

> My back hurt like hell and I couldn't carry no more, but I went on and on, all evening. When I finally was finished, I walked into the kitchen and there was just this huge pile of dishes... so I just walked right on out. Man, that was just unreal, you know, she just can't do that!

The "she" John refers to Andrea, the manager of the hotel. Art has also heard about her that she "exploits people mercilessly," as he describes, although according to his own words he has never been inside the Grand.

Many months go by without John ever working again. And he never manages to get any genuine friends other than me the way Art does, and that is probably why he eventually decides to go to New York. Just before John is about to leave for New York, he wants me to help him find a job there. "Just some day labor," he instructs me. He is especially interested in what the wages are going to be, so we find a chart on minimum wages across the country. The fact that the minimum wage in New York also is 5.15 USD[3] disappoints John, and we have to find the information on several different pages until John accepts it as fact. "Shit, for that money I don't even think I want to work at all!" John bursts out. Instead he plans to sleep on a park bench in Central Park. "I only want to stay there till October anyways," he tells me, "then it'll get cold." His airplane ticket to New York is for early June.

When leaving (see also — "Leaving Town", p. 191), John puts all he wants to take into a big sack and a cardboard box and then he uses a shopping cart to push it all around town. The bus station is located at the border, and we agree that I go down there with

---

[3]The state of New York has since decided on a state minimum wage of 6.00 USD starting January 1st 2005, but several industries are exempted.

him and then return with his keys; so I can take everything I want from his apartment before the landlord gets there.

When John has left, I walk back to his apartment, and there is everything! The refrigerator is filled up with groceries he has bought a few days before, and beer is left there also. He left a poster I had given him, and all his jackets and shoes other than those that he is wearing, are still there. All his mail between late January and early June is packed in a cardboard box that is stuffed in a corner of his living room. And all his bank and credit cards lay cut up in a few big pieces on the kitchen counter. A quick scan of his mail makes it clear: he owes the gas company money and has two credit card companies on his heels. It took one of the companies two and a half months to find him here in Douglas, but since then they have been relentless. They even had offered settlements where he would have to pay only 600 USD on a credit card bill of several thousands, but John did not pay, because he did not even have that amount available. For John, leaving obviously meant trying to start his life over, and so he left everything behind. How many times he has been doing that before, I do not know.

A feature unique to John is that he believes he can buy himself out of a friendship by giving away some consumer goods. For example, there is the situation when John suddenly gets angry with Art a few months into his stay, because Art helps him transport a sofa to his place they disagree with the way they should tie it to the car's roof. John then decides to end the friendship. He does that by taking the kitchen utensils that Art had stored at his place over to the Lerman and also a number of food items that he had prepared in advance to give to Art. "You know, I think it's a bit risky having him over here; he seems kind of like a shaky character," John explains his buy-out afterwards. At another time, he surprises Todd by showing up at his house with some wine and chicken one night. This time it is about trying to build a relationship, and probably is also part of a scheme to get access to the job opportunities that both he and Art believe Todd has.

For John, his money is something that comes directly from the United States government, regardless of where he is living or how much he works. This is slightly different from Mr. Fernandez, who is only receiving government money indirectly through his

Photo: unknown

Picture 8: Art and the telescope that will save the Douglas economy. Picture taken at a shelter in New Mexico, Art's car is in the background.

customers. While one would think that it might result in a very nationally bounded conceptualization, once again the concept of citizenship, which is so closely connected to it, apparently does not make sense to John. A lot may have to do with his fleeing from debt, which, he believes can be avoided if one only moves on quick enough.

John also builds up connections to others by sharing various gifts on a local level. However, John uses money from the U.S. government in his close surroundings, paying back the debts of canceled friendships or investing in other friendships. And because his close surroundings constantly shift, and therefore his U.S. dollars function as universal money, that can be used anywhere, his money does not build up any localized definition of community.

Art

Art Caveny is very frugal with his money and that is why he initially decides to stay in his car, despite the reasonable (180 USD/month) pricing of the Posada Lerman. It is only when John, Mr. Fernandez, and I arrange for a Christian agency to pay his rent for the first month, with Art having to add only 20 USD to make up for an extra week's worth of rent, that he decides to move in. Mr. Fernandez reacts upon hearing that the rent Art got for the first week is about to run out. The two of us stand on the back porch of the Lerman one rainy night talking about how to stabilize the financial situation of the various inhabitants. Mr. Fernandez' suggestion is to "just tell him [Art] to go to the Arizona office there [pointing across the dimly lid parking lot to the Arizona Department of Economic Security office] and tell them I sent him." Art believes it is a bad idea because he is afraid to claim to live anywhere else than California, due to his fear that it may diminish his chances to receive funding from that particular state for one of his projects.

Art does have access to Arizona Food stamps (147 USD/month) though, and he makes full use of them. I exchange some of my dollars for food that he buys with his food stamps in the early months I am there. Art spends the money on gas for his car. He manages to pay rent with various income sources. A few weeks after moving into the Lerman, he receives 400 USD from his mother, he works one night as a security guard for an annual event held by the library in the park (see p. 33), and he works for a few months cleaning toilets in the hotel.

During the last few months of my first stay, Art tries to apply for a government grant from the state of California to build a glider-powered windmill. I help him fill out the budget, but it is his plan. Bruce and I take the initiative to try to get the Danish or Norwegian universities interested in him, but unfortunately without any luck. He goes pretty far with his application in California, but is ultimately denied the grant, and on my second visit, he is talking with Stan about filing a more professional application next time.

Art's concept of money is highly theoretical and very much separate from his own access to it. He has read a lot on various subjects, including economics. He is a big fan of Adam Smith, and it is his theory that we are living under a form of monopolism rather than capitalism that determines most of his ideas on money. Part of his drive to invent a new windmill system is that the heavy use of wind energy will enable an energy infrastructure that has a broader base of ownership than a system based on oil possibly could because oil has such a high capital cost.

He also has a number of other favorite subjects related to money that he presents to his listeners at the library, such as a new style of housing that can be built very cheap, but is forbidden according to the U.S. building codes, and how he would combine the mass building of that new style of housing in Jordan and other countries surrounding Israel with indebtedness schemes for those deciding to live in them, in order to create a lasting peace in the Middle East. All of his schemes usually have in common the idea that some technical solution will create huge social and economic improvements.

When we go out to eat at the churches (see — "Getting to know one another", p. 17), I leave early from the last church, and head over to the library, since it opens at 1pm, so I do not get to see the end of the meeting. Art shows up about an hour later. "Maybe their budget will hold next year when some of them have earned a few 100,000 dollars — thanks to me," he says joyfully when he enters. When Art is about to build the prototype for a new windmill a few months later, Jeff reports that Art tells him that he really does not need to go to school any longer, as he will find work in Art's windmill factory.

Also Art presents himself as potentially very rich. According to him, his grandfather opened a fund in 1920 that would "pan out" in 2020. If Art is still alive by then, he will have to share the approximate sum of 1 Billion USD with many others, but he will get a minimum of 10 million USD as his inheritance.

Art stands out a little in that he sees the state of California as a major source of possible access to money. In his application for the grant he goes as far as talking about the "first mover" situation that California will be able to profit from, if they invest in his research project. This places Art into the same category as Stern (2004) as both see California as being a 'frontier,' not only of the United States in relation to Mexico, but also in relation to technological progress. However, for Art the boundaries of California are floating and the

Internet has given him the possibility to be part of groups there while staying in Arizona. On the other hand, his ideas of trying to start a factory in Douglas shows that he does not see why a city in Arizona should have any less chance than one in California of building up a totally new industry.

However, as his story about Jordan shows, for him money is not national or local but a completely global affair — although from a very pro-capitalist viewpoint.

Zack

Zack Perez is one of the first persons I meet. Simultaneously, he has mainly five economic concerns in terms of spending:

The monthly payments of his fine: His release from prison has been conducted on the provision that he will pay off a fine over a period of 18 months.

His burned down house and the rebuilding of it: He has been contacted by the city because there is trash all over his property during his first few days at the Lerman. Also, he wants to rebuild the inside of his house to be able to live in it again and save on the rent.

Rent and Food and other regular payments: In contrast to Art and John, Zack cannot apply for Food Stamps because he has to have a constant income to satisfy his other obligations.

Drugs: The reason Zack had ended up in prison to begin with is that he needed money for drugs. His urge for drugs has not stopped since he got out, although he tries to suppress it by studying the Bible extensively.

His future wife: Shortly after I move out of the Posada Lerman, he marries his wife who is still living in New Mexico, although she promises to move to Douglas once the house is done. Even though Zack is in desperate need for money during their wedding in Douglas, she is mostly a source of income for him, since she has a regular job and can provide him with gifts of money that are wired through from New Mexico.

During the first days I was at the Posada Lerman, Zack tries to get back with his old employer. According to Zack, he has been promised that he will get his old job back again if he gets out of prison. But now that he is out, every day his employer keeps telling him that there is no work. And when he finally does get out working on a site at the border to New Mexico, he gets less pay than he had gotten before. "Why doesn't he just tell me that he found someone else to do the job?" Zack frequently wonders in the evenings when we are all gathered on the sofa in the lobby of the Lerman, in front of the television.

Zack is very open about his budgeting and how much he has earned. Once, he makes the entire calculation of money while pacing back and forth between me and the TV. He recognizes that even if he has to work for the low pay he is now getting, he would be able to have about 20–50 USD left for rebuilding the house after paying everything else. His drugs and future wife and her kids are not considered as a cost factor in the calculation. The drug deal that got him into prison to begin with would have given him 23,000 USD, according to what he tells me.

The relationship that the others of us have with Zack turns sour when he starts asking to borrow money. First, he borrows five dollars from John, and then he borrows five dollars from me. After I have moved out of the Lerman, he knocks on the front door of Todd's house, where I am staying by myself at the time, and asks for another 20 dollars. It is about 10pm on the night before his bride is going to arrive in Douglas for their wedding. He says that he needs to buy wedding rings and that he has seen some for 20 dollars in a store on G Avenue. I tell him I am very short on money myself and he begs me to lend him at least 10 dollars so he can get the store owner to hold the rings for him. I decide to lend him 15 dollars. He also offers his wallet me to keep until he has returned the money, but it occurs to me later that he probably just had said that without meaning it, because he does not renew the offer after we have gone to Circle K together, where I need to break a twenty dollar bill. He tells me that he will return the money the next morning.

When I walk over to the Lerman the next morning, Zack is gone. John suggests that he has probably left for work and so I come back in the late afternoon the same day when I know he has finished work. I am sitting on the couch beside John when Zack's girlfriend calls from a cell phone on the outskirts of Douglas. I then ask for my money, and Zack gets angry with me because I am so "rude about it," but he gives me back my 15 dollars before his bride enters the Lerman. However, John never sees his money again. When his bride arrives, she has her two kids and an aunt with her. John asks whether he is allowed to give the kids some cookies, and he is allowed to do so, although their mother reminds them that they are to go out to eat in a little while. Knowing Zack's financial situation, it makes me feel very uncomfortable for having demanded him to repay the 15 dollars just 10 minutes earlier.

Zack is clearly unique in his economic situation; for him it is the U.S. government that takes money away, while it is the border area that provides the opportunities to earn money and spend it on worthwhile activities. In this way, Zack is regionalized in his understanding of money and monetary networks. Zack stands out from the others at the Lerman in that he has access to a large network of contacts which he potentially can use in order to acquire the necessities of life. In modern day sociology this kind of power that Zack holds is called 'social capital.' Social capital can be accumulated and is somewhat independent of the amount of economical capital one holds. It consists of the lasting network of resources through controlled by acquaintances that one possibly can mobilize in ones own favor. And the fact that most of Zack's contacts live in Douglas means that his access to material wealth is very much connected to the local (Bourdieu 1986).

However, I think it would be going too far to say that Zack mainly defines network through locally produced items. Sure — a large percentage of his consumption is local, and his networks of friends are stimulated through the use of money, but his girlfriend and her income-producing job are in a distant location, and the consumer food items that he buys have not been mentioned, because they are what just about everyone else in Douglas consumes — the cheapest version of the globally produced products that Food City carries.

Joe

Joe lives well outside of Douglas, but several of my informants deal a lot with him, because he has been for some time a major source of employment for several of them — or rather they hope that he will be. Travels out of Douglas are not normal for most of my informants, but travels to Joe's are an exception. When considering the limits of an economic exchange network, I therefore find it natural to include him.

Joe is living more than an hour's car ride from Douglas and a substantial part of this journey is on a dirt road. He bought his property while in Wilcox in the late seventies or early eighties with the money of a very rich girlfriend he had at the time, which they carried in a suitcase. Other than that, he has not had access to much money for the years since then.

Recently John Smith, a new neighbor, has moved in. He is the former CEO of a major national computer corporation, and he has helped Joe apply for a government grant for an environmental project to preserve the flow in a nearby creek (the area is called Turkey Creek). The creek gets water from the mountains around it, and the water used to flow all year, despite the fact that it usually only rains during a few summer months. After cattle have been overgrazing the mountains for several years, the water flowing down the mountains has increased in speed so it runs only for a short while. The idea of the project is to decrease the speed of the water by inserting hundreds of small dams in the waterbed. The dams are built by hand and without the use of many tools. They are made of rocks and the workers are mainly Mexicans with Green Cards.

Joe has a job there as project manager and he earns around 15 USD per hour at the job while workers get 8 USD per hour and the foreman gets 8.5 USD per hour.

Joe's concept of money is closely connected to his general idea of how the world is constituted. His main criticism of American society is that it is too consumer focused. He also believes in the Marxist concept of 'exploitation' of workers. This kind of thinking spurred his decision to move out to his present location. He also shows me how he tries to stay true to his condemnation of exploitation while at the same time employing Mexican workers — by telling me how one of his billionaire neighbors tried to lower the wages of the workers to 3 USD per hour.

Joe also has the government as a major source of income, although in a different way. However, he shares with Art a more theoretical concept of money that is probably quite different than how he actually uses it. On the labor market, Mexican workers are paid substantially less than U.S. workers; however Joe does not entirely accept the rules of the market. Although Joe does not have any financial connection with the world outside North America, to him Arizona is clearly a part of the United States.

Todd

Todd Daniels is indebted when I meet him, because he has a fine that he got for smuggling illegal immigrants across the border into the U.S., which he is trying to pay off. Therefore, in addition to his job at El Espejo (see p. 24), he takes on a job with a good friend of Kevin's — Joe. Todd is not the foreman, but he is the only one on the project fluent in both Spanish and English and Joe only speaks English, so Todd becomes the natural communication link between Joe and the workers. For a few weeks he lives out at Joe's place but they do not get along and Todd is fired and returns to Douglas to work at El Espejo once again. I am at Joe's during the next-to-last week that Todd is there, and during the last week Todd and Bruce are working there together, so I hear the details from them.

During Todd's last week on the job, John Smith, who speaks Spanish and has a stake in the project as well, comes for a visit and tells the workers that the dams need to be much higher. Peter, the inspector for the project, is supposed to come out to make a determination, but they cancel that because it will be very expensive. Todd disagrees strongly, because he views the workers as professionals at their work, and he believes that they will know best how high the dams need to be. Joe lets the workers figure out how to build the dams themselves, and they have made much faster progress than the plan calls for, during the month that Todd is on the job. While John is out there, he wants to control every detail of the work, having Todd and Bruce mark all the positions where check dams are to be built, instead of letting the workers decide as they go along. Todd thinks that if he is to do work that he is not in control of, he ought to get higher wages. At that point, Joe accuses Todd of trying to unionize the workers, although he agrees that it might not be a good idea to make the check dams higher.

When I have some trouble with John McConnell back in Douglas a few weeks later (see — "John's got a gun", p. 123), I stay with Bruce at Joe's one Monday until the following Wednesday after work. During this time, John Smith sends over instructions on paper in Spanish from his other home in Massachusetts, telling them that they are "in big trouble" because the dams are unnecessarily high. Now they are at risk of losing their grant, and John Smith argues with the grant-givers by e-mail, until they send an e-mail canceling the project. The next day they call Joe and tell him the project is still on as long as John Smith stays out of it and Peter monitors it closely. Joe is embarrassed that the workers will have to rebuild the dams, but they say they do not mind, as long as they get paid.

Todd's concept of wages for work that one does not control fits Marx's idea of alienation. According to Marx, the problem of wage work is two-fold. Firstly, the worker receives a lower wage than the capitalist profits on the work done (Marx 1999, 142); secondly the worker is alienated from his own product if he does not control it himself. It is "the domination of the thing over man, of dead labour over living labour, of the product over the producer" (Marx 1999, 383).

Todd initially asks me to pay 75 USD/month rent and I continue to stay at his house for this price for a few more months. This covers expenses for water and electricity and gives him approximately an additional 25 USD. For a while, he tries to find another job, but finally gives up paying off his debt by working. Instead, he applies for money from the same source that John is receiving it. He also says that if only he waits it out until the next spring, he will not have to pay off the entire fine in order to be able to leave the U.S.

Todd also presents himself as very rich. He tells me that he made a lot of money during his time in Vietnam, and he put a large portion of it in the Cayman Islands. He cannot get to it there, and that was the point of putting it there — he does not trust himself with his money.

Todd's concept of money is close to that of Art's: he is very critical of the current society, but does not believe in non-market solutions. Todd uses most of his time at El Espejo to read books critical of Bush or the U.S. government, and comments on them whenever visitors come by. A lot of his criticism revolves around the U.S.'s refusal to support democracies and free markets, its stand in favor of monopolism, and its implicit policy of overthrowing governments around the world.

The thing that distinguishes Todd from the Lerman crowd is not so much that he has more money. In fact, he probably has access to less. Nevertheless, he is viewed upon by John and Art as an important contact to have and they are both more interested in getting into contact with him than he is in having anything to do with them. But Todd is much better read and knows quite a bit about both Mexico and other foreign cultures. In the terminology of Bourdieu (1986), he would have a lot of what is called 'cultural capital.' Cultural capital is simply any kind of education or skill that sets one apart from the rest of society because they give status. For Todd it also means having to promote his extra education, as with the current labor situation he can not covert his cultural capital into a job that would pay more than what other workers receive.

Bruce

Bruce had finished his studies in Europe a few years earlier and worked in London for some time after graduating. Three months before I arrive, he had gone to his parents for what he thought would be a short visit. But when I leave, he is still there, and finally leaves after a 10-month stay. For several months, he is planning to get a position as a stringer for *Voice of America* and a few other media programs in Nigeria, but in the end he gives up on that plan and goes to Nepal, about two months after I leave.

Bruce's plan is to earn 4–5 thousand USD before leaving, to have a safe base to start from. He begins by trying to find employment in nearby Tucson, where his brother Robert works as a chef in a

gourmet restaurant. However, he does not find any work there, so
he ends up getting employment at the environmental project. Bruce
does not speak Spanish fluently when he starts working, but his
French helps him to improve it rapidly through interaction with the
workers, and the timing is such that he is able to take over Todd's
position as translator when Joe fires Todd. And although he clearly
is "over-educated" for the job, he does not see anything degrading
in the work itself. He also knows that he will not have to work on
the rock dams for the rest of his life, while the others, all in their
fifties and sixties with the oldest being 66 year old Norberto, have
worked up to 35 years on similar physical work.

Bruce's spending clearly differs from the other workers in that
he saves it for one special event while the others spend it for immediate consumption. But Bruce can also draw on his education
and family to obtain money in a way the other workers cannot. For
example, he borrows one of his parents' cars, paying only for the
gas, and goes to Tucson to visit Robert over the weekend. And
when Joe's wife suddenly has to step down from her position as a
councilor in Tucson, Bruce is given a week off to write an article
about it for the Tucson Weekly — with full pay for half the time.

In the eyes of Todd, Joe, and Bruce, the foreman Jose at the
environmental project turns more and more corrupt. "They say
he has a fifteen year old girlfriend who is very demanding," is the
explanation both Bruce and Todd give me. While Todd is working
there, John Smith gets a call from Joe asking for money to help
one of his family members who is allegedly in prison. John says
he cannot do anything about it, but he also calls Joe to tell him.
Todd asks Jose about it the next day, and Jose cuts the conversation
short, stating that the person is out of prison already. "A typical
Mexican story," Todd remarks. He does not believe it. Also, Jose
writes the paychecks for the workers, and during the one week
when Todd and Bruce are working there together, they calculate
that he is taking a percentage of each workers pay in addition to
his own wage which is already 50 cents an hour higher than the
others.

Unlike Todd, Bruce does not want to live out there, at least
for quite a few weeks. Instead he drives in with the workers each
morning. He quickly notices that Jose is also charging the others

considerably more for the gas than the regular gas price and he also asks to borrow money without ever repaying it. The truck that they are driving, which Bruce thought was Jose's, is really paid for by one of the other workers without Jose ever paying it back. Hearing that, Joe calls Jose "your jefe" whenever speaking to Bruce.

After a few weeks, Jose asks Bruce to translate for him, and he instructs the crew that they will henceforth start working at 5am instead of 7am, which means he will have to meet them at the border at 3am. And they also want to work on the weekends, but they are told that they cannot work during the weekends because they already work 40 hours and so any extra time would have to be paid overtime at 150% salary. Jose then asks whether they can work for a regular 100% salary. Because the project is a government project, it cannot be done, so instead they are allowed to work for one of the property owners in Turkey Creek during the weekends. Bruce turns down the work during the weekends though, even though it would mean that he would be able to save money for his trip faster.

Bruce is planning to spend the money he earns globally, even more so than all the other informants. I can see that it places him in a different category than other workers, and it is his initial class background that lets him quickly advance to more enjoyable employment opportunities. However, his financial needs and the amount that he earns are actually lower than that of the Mexican workers! It is interesting to see that among a large proportion of the Douglasites, there is no direct connection between income and class, at least among the lower classes (lower proletariat, lumpenproletariat, etc.).

Soerlie

I first meet Soerlie, a very openly gay retired music teacher from Oklahoma, when Todd sees him outside the windows of La Gardin as we are eating there early one morning. After Soerlie has ignored Todd's knocking on the window for about half a minute, Todd jumps to the door and asks Soerlie to step inside. "Do you know where I have been this morning?" Soerlie blurts out aggressively, "I have been walking all the way from Southwest Medical Center!" (a few kilometers outside of town). "My finger is about to fall off." he says, showing his badly wounded hand. He continues to complain for a few minutes, while getting inappropriately impatient with the staff. "It's all the crack I'm smoking," he half-whispers, "... but I need it, it's the only medicine that helps ... it takes the pain away." Then he turns more positive and continues: "You know, the desert is not good for my skin, but when the sun goes over the mountain tops in the mornings [sniff] ... it's beautiful!"

The next subject concerns whether or not he should rent a house that he has found in Agua Prieta. The rent is 400 USD/month and he is considering it, but wonders whether the price is too high. He gets a monthly check of 2500 USD, which Todd tells me after Soerlie has left (Soerlie has shown it to him). Soerlie cannot live where he has been living, because he owes some crack dealers some money "and last night they ganged up on [him]" and trashed the place where he lives. His belongings are still there though.

So far he has only been talking to Todd, even though I am sitting at the same table, but as his burrito arrives, he notices me. "Who is your young companion?" he addresses Todd. When Todd tells him that I am from a number of European countries including Germany, Soerlie lightens considerably up: "Ahhh! Salzburg und Wien, lalalala..." (singing a few notes of a song which I probably am supposed to recognize but do not, while smiling broadly). He has been in Europe and especially liked Salzburg, Austria. He despises Americans for not appreciating the Arts and immediately assumes that I do, since I am European. We talk about the war with Iraq and Todd tells him that he is against the current war and about how U.S. foreign policy has been "bad" for at least the past century, and then he adds, "This young fellow [me] is a socialist." "I am with you all the way, it's the only way!" Soerlie says quickly and decisively, and continues on about how he is a communist and that he stopped hiding it any longer, just as he is not hiding that he is gay or a "crack head".

With a newfound smile, Soerlie reconsiders the rent for the house. "I will do it!" he exclaims, "I have been paying that much in Oklahoma. [...] Yeah, I can afford that." But first Soerlie checks the time. Although he is not religious he wants to go to all the churches this morning to get them to give him some money to pay the initial rent with. Soerlie is excited, and he sneers:

> I can cry on command [...] Sometimes I go across the border late at night when everything is closed and tell the border guards that I have just entered the United States and don't have any money for the night right now as I'm still waiting for my things to arrive. Then they give me 20 dollars and I ... [with gestures he shows that he walks right back across the border and uses the money to buy crack]

It is 10am, and Soerlie leaves for his church visits.

A few days later, I meet Soerlie at El Espejo while talking to Kevin. "They have been trying to kill me last night," he announces. "And I'm not laughing either," he adds as Kevin is overtly smiling at his comment. Soerlie explains that he barely escaped as they were trying to cut off his finger. His skin is looking much better in general though, and Todd comments on that. It puts Soerlie back in a cheerful mood and he leaves. "They have been trying to kill me last night," Kevin mocks Soerlie's earlier comment, "I just can't help laughing when he says that shit. He is just so full of it."

For the next few weeks I meet Soerlie every now and then either at El Espejo or in town and he starts wearing a chain of wooden beads that looks like it may have come from a Mardi Gras celebration or something similar. At nighttime he likes to hang around the Circle K, and in the daytime one can catch him at El Espejo. He usually complains about almost getting killed, but nothing really happens for the next few weeks.

Then one evening I am walking to the Lerman Hotel with Art after the library has closed, since he is supposed to make food that night. It is at the time when John has just found the job at the Grand Hotel washing dishes and he has lent us the key to his room (see also p. 51). Art still lives in #13 and John in #5. Art starts off by telling me that "the new guy is real openly gay and I don't think John noticed yet." I had not heard of any new tenant, so I ask Art for further details. He tells the story:

> Last night there was an old man coming in here and he asked whether he could stay here for 20 dollars that he

had gotten from the St. Vincent De Paul's. Mr. Fernandez told him that it would bring him through the first hour. The old guy didn't get the joke and was about to get epileptic spasms when he heard that. You know, he has real bad arthritis and had a hard time walking already before that, but after that he was really about to fall apart. He has been living in AP, but he says that the neighbor kids have been throwing rocks through his windows and made one huge mess of his house over there.

It is not hard to figure out who has moved into my old #6. And he shows up later while we are making food in Art's room: "Ah, Art is cooking, I see...and our young Austrian friend is here as well." He dances a few steps from a Broadway play (he explains later). He is carrying a plastic bag with a few things from his house in Agua Prieta. He leads me into his room while he is talking, and the first thing he picks out of the bag is a picture of Salzburg that he puts on the table, which is leaning against the wall, because he does not have any tools to mount it on the wall. He explains that the kids have been vandalizing his house and that he is now moving over here and that he likes the room a lot. And 200 USD/month is not too bad either. I offer to help him move his things. He accepts my offer politely and we agree to meet the next day at 10am, and he adds: "And you know, mi casa es su casa...but now, I need some time alone," and he shows me out of the room with a swift move of his cane. When he opens the door again a few minutes later, Art asks him whether he would like some food. Soerlie accepts, and I hand him a plastic bowl. He closes his door immediately and when he opens it again, the bowl has been washed and two fortune cookies have been placed inside of it. He hands it to us, drags out the pronunciation of the word "cookies," and goes back into his room without saying another word.

The next morning, at the time we agreed to meet, Soerlie is not there. But there is a note hanging on the door saying: "Johannes, I had to go to AP already. Meet me instead at 3pm here." Underneath that he has drawn a few notes and labeled it "Austrian national anthem." I have other plans at 3pm that day, so I never get to see his house in AP.

The last time any of us see Soerlie is when he suddenly drives up with a red sports car at El Espejo: "I've had enough, I'm off to Oklahoma now, I just had to get someone to sponsor new tires for this one, but now it's done — 350 dollars." He wants to give his last Mexican coins to anyone who will take them, as he is "through with Mexico." He drives off and Kevin remarks: "I wonder how long he will stay away [...] last week he was off to New York." But we never do see Soerlie again. According to Todd and Kevin, he had come to Douglas in a totally different car than the one that he had driven off in.

Soerlie combines many of the characteristics of Zack and John: his environment shifts even faster than that of John and he has income from the U.S. government. He also has somehow managed to acquire enough localized knowledge to know how to extract money from the area just like Zack does. His spending habits can also be compared to that of John in that he uses it to build up local networks and acquire goods that he will have to leave behind. He also has no bounded local economic network.

Sarah and Tom

Sarah and her husband Tom Barker, the parents of Bruce, are known in Douglas as the librarian and her husband. They clearly have access to more money than most Douglasites and most people I actually meet, but they are very much aware that it is only relatively so. Earlier in their life, they worked for over a decade as teachers in Australia but came back to be closer to Sarah's family in the southeastern U.S. . This resulted in a major cut in their wages, to such an extent that their children could apply for subsidized lunches for the first few years when Sarah stayed home with the children.

According to their story, when they had returned to the U.S., Tom had quit many jobs without considering the economic consequences, while Sarah had been working steadily to ensure a steady family income. They insisted on letting me stay for free in their RV for the last two months of my stay, even though I offered to pay some kind of rent.

How much money they exactly have is much more difficult for me to determine than for just about anyone around the Lerman, it seems. It is an interesting phenomenon in that Kevin's, and to a certain extent Todd's access to money is also unknown to everybody else.

Unlike the two other places that I stay, the Barkers' house is not located downtown, but in a more affluent neighborhood some ten blocks from the inner city. Close to their home is the low-priced grocery store Food City, that most from the Lerman reach by a free bus that runs from the border, through the inner city and then to Food City on a very uncertain schedule about every half-hour. This grocery store is not good enough for the Barkers, so instead they go to Safeway, which is located about 500m on the other side of the city center. Safeway is quite a bit more expensive, but they carry a greater variety of breads and a various other items.

Having lived outside the United States, the Barkers feel that they can speak about economics from a broader perspective. "Americans don't realize what rights they really should have," Sarah says one day when talking about the small amount of vacation that Americans generally have. Also, they are critical of the economic policies of the U.S. . "If you want to ask the government for money in this country, you need to build weapons or something," Sarah says at La Gardin (see p. 30) one Sunday morning, when talking about Art's chances to receive money from a grant or some other government program. Also Tom explains that Cuba is being strangled by the U.S. embargo, and he tries to convince one of his friends to go there with him — some time before he is to die.

The Barkers represent another case of money coming from the government (through Sarah's job as librarian), but it does not have much influence on their attitudes toward the government, nor does it foster an understanding of a closed national money circuit; money is something that is handed out by various governments, and some governments are better than others — with the U.S. being among the worst. The Barker's clearly hold the most basic kind of capital, economic capital, which she has been able to convert from her education as a librarian (cultural capital) and which is also helping

Photo: Johannes Wilm

Picture 9: Bicycle Peter in his trailer in the United States

her in building up a social network (social capital) (Bourdieu 1986). Had their income been the same, but relatively less compared to that of other income groups in town, this last conversion would not have been possible.

It is also interesting to see that the difference in class (Sarah is employed by the government rather than receiving unemployment benefits), has little consequence on their understanding of economics.

Bicycle Peter

Bicycle Peter is constantly out of money, but he tries to give away as much as possible to others who are even more in need of it and who do not have access to the same benefits that he has, since they usually lack either U.S. citizenship, English skills, or both. Around 70 years old, Peter spends most of his two monthly checks on the house he has in Agua Prieta for the first several months of my stay, and on a prostitute in Chihuahua, a few hours south of Douglas, who is about forty years younger than he is. She repeatedly promises to use the money to buy bus tickets to Agua Prieta for herself and her daughter, but never follows through. During annual *National Library Week*, Peter mostly survives on the free cookies the library gives out. Then for about 10 days, he subsists on a bag of rice that Kevin has given him. Kevin says he always tries to give Peter a drink when he comes in, just to make sure eats something every day. One time when I am certain he has not eaten anything for the last 24 hours, Bruce and I conspire with the staff at La Gardin to give him a free meal without telling him where the money has come from. "Did he know someone is paying for him?" Michelle asks afterwards, "He didn't even ask for the bill, and he ate as if he hadn't been eating for like a week!"

A few weeks earlier, Peter wishes to sell his bike for 60 USD in order to buy a bus ticket to Chihuahua. I tell him that I will see whether I can help him sell his bike. The next day he waits at El Espejo all day for me to show up. When I hear that night that he has been waiting for me the entire working day, I decide to pawn his bike for 60 USD the next day, after he assures me he has an agreement with a bike shop in AP to borrow another bike for the time being. When I see him walking around town a few days later and he tells me that the bike shop has moved far from the border into Agua Prieta, so that he cannot get a bike after all, I immediately give him the bike back. He insists on paying back the 60 USD and shows up with the money a few weeks later, but also tells me that he is in immediate need of exactly 60 USD. I give him the money back and never see it again.

To earn some money, Peter plans to start working for an insurance company in Douglas as he has done before. He cannot work in Mexico because he would have to apply for status as an immigrant, and he does not have enough money to show that he would not be "a burden to the Mexican government." He has come into contact with one insurance company that he used to work for, and he has bought a list of names and addresses of 5,260 of people 60 years of age and older living in Douglas that he can send cards out to. The first time I am at his house, he tells me how the insurance company's plan to recruit people is as effective as "throw[ing] it out of a helicopter": They plan to mail the cards out to everyone on the list and then to wait for the cards to be sent back to the company headquarters, which will then notify Peter of the prospects who have shown interest. Peter decides instead to mail the cards to a select few of the prospects on his own, and then visit them two or three days later. As he currently does not have a car, he will instead ride his bike around. And since it is dangerous to ride at night, he will have to restrict himself to Saturdays and Sundays during the daytime. He tells me he also needs to hide the bike, because people will not trust a person who arrives on a bike.

When I visit Peter two months later, he has moved to the United States and given up his plan of selling insurance policies his own way. "I tried visiting a few but it didn't work," he explains with a resigned voice. Instead he has decided to follow the company model.

Half a year later, when I am back in Douglas, Peter is once again trying his own plan. Now he has printed out the addresses. His daughter from somewhere far up north, who has been visiting him, has arranged for him to get his teeth fixed at the dentist so he looks presentable when trying to sell the insurance. "Now all I need is the stamps," is Peter's conclusion.

Peter is in many ways similar to Art in that he has a business plan that just never comes to fruition. And also, just like Art's plans, it involves channeling money into Douglas from other locations in the U.S. However, there are also differences — while Art sees the power of cheap labor in Douglas and he is going for government money, Peter sees Douglas mainly as a market and is going for money from the private sector.

There is also the difference that Peter moves across the border and has a lot more knowledge of Mexico than Art. He is a prime example of a person that tries to use his knowledge of both cultures in order to convert the relatively small amount of money he receives in the United States into a relatively higher amount in Mexico. He is not the only one, but one of very few that I have seen that try to climb the class ladder by going to Mexico — the vast majority tries to do it by going in the opposite direction.

Garry Mora

Garry Mora, the Korean owner of California Pizza, gives me his opinion about the differences among the races: "We Asians work very hard, and you White people also work very hard, and also Mexicans work very hard, but Black people, they don't work. They sleep." A few days later, he tries to get me into a fraudulent pyramid scheme that sells Mangosteen juice. "You could retire very soon," he tries to convince me, "and be a millionaire!"

My immediate reaction is that he is probably being taken in by it himself, so I ask him how he learned about it. His connection to the Mangosteen network is through another Asian in his fifties who is just about to walk in through the door right then. He has a convertible outside, wears a nice suit and has a cell phone in his pocket that is connected to a headset with a microphone. He briefly nods at me, thinking that I am probably a prospective client, and he tells Garry Mora that he does not have much time, because he needs to go back to "the conference next door"[4]. After he is gone, I tell Garry that he should probably try to get out of the scheme if he can do it without too much of an economic loss. He partially agrees, but he says he first wants to try it out himself. Several months later, I learn from Sarah that Garry is running an unofficial loan agency with very high interest rates, and so I conclude he is not quite as innocent in the Mangosteen scheme as he tries to look.

The example here is quite telling: Garry Mora's primary concern is the sale of an Asian fruit product through a network of local Asians. The economy is global and so is money — although it is unevenly distributed, because of the different amount of work that each person is willing to do. Therefore unlike most others, he endorses the way money is currently flowing and he has a strong belief in the system as it is.

Garry is probably the only one that I meet in Douglas who is really in the private small business owner class and who actually makes a living from it.

---

[4]California Pizza is close to the Grand, so that is where I imagine he goes.

Maria

One and a half months after I leave the first time, the high school graduate Maria quits her job at the library and gets a full-time position at Wal-Mart. The old Wal-Mart is to be replaced by a Super Wal-Mart directly across the street, a few months after I leave. The building project of the enormous new Wal-Mart Superstore is one of the main themes of conversation in all segments of society during my first stay. Maria is first employed by Wal-Mart at the old store, but many new workers are employed at about the same time, in order to prepare for the transition.

At first, Maria's pay goes down to 5.40 USD an hour from the 5.60 USD an hour she was receiving at the library, but she works a full 40 hours a week, so she will end up with 216 USD a week instead of 110 USD a week. After a week, on her first day off, she tells me she has been working 42 hours, and she is "not sure" whether she will get time and a half[5] for the last two hours. She will also have no health insurance coverage for the first six months, "just in case I quit or whatnot." But she will get a pay raise after the first month of .75 USD an hour.

Instead of having to pay for Maria's health insurance, Wal-Mart chooses to fire her on the 28th of December, shortly before she reaches the six-month mark. According to Maria, they fire 40 employees all at once, and their goal is to fire 200–300 of the initial 500 employees at the new Wal-Mart Superstore. In addition to the health insurance benefits, her salary would have gone up to 6.80 USD an hour if she had kept working.

When I talk to Maria about two weeks after she has been fired, she is quite disappointed. We watch MTV that morning and she chats on the Internet during the commercial breaks while we discuss the subject. Although she is quite aware of the economics involved, she laments: "The managers told me they wanted me to become a cashier and then a CSM[6]."

Then she starts reflecting on her time at Wal-Mart. While she was still at the old Wal-Mart, she got paid overtime, but when she

---

[5]In the U.S. it is a general rule that you get paid 1.5 times the normal salary for any overtime.

[6]Customer Service Manager

moved over to the new Wal-Mart, she only was able to work 32 hours a week. By the end of November she was down to 25 hours, and eventually she was "getting paid for 20 hours, but actually worked 30 hours." This was around Christmas and "they wanted gift cards to be the number one selling item, so [she] started pushing them." Nevertheless, "it still was a good job" in her view.

Pushing gift cards is not the only thing on her track record at Wal-Mart that Maria is proud of. She feels that she had been well-liked at Wal-Mart, and proudly tells me how a customer once complimented her: "I have been shopping for two hours and you are the first person I see with a smile."

When asking what she wants to do next in her life, she admits that she really wishes she would be rehired. "Curtis, he knew my name [...] and he is a co-manager." A few weeks later, her wish comes true and she e-mails me, proudly telling me that she has been rehired.

Most of all, Maria is part of a U.S. proletariat. However, considering the uncertainty that is connected with her job, she might be categorized in a subdivision of the lumpenproletariat that is sometimes able to work. For Maria, the job at Wal-Mart led her into contact with Mexico and the United States at the same time: her shadowy corporate management is somewhere in the United States, and her customers are mainly from Mexico. Moreover, most of the production of the goods being sold is probably taking place in Asia.

Jeff and January

Two other high school graduates are the couple Jeff and January. Jeff's father is a psychologist, his mother is a teacher, and both of January's parents are doctors. Both January and Jeff live in Douglas, but January's parents work in Agua Prieta.

Jeff says he believes in capitalism. Concerning his girlfriend's parents, he says: "Why should it be someone else's burden that her parents work in Mexico, and make so little?" Jeff is not alone in that assessment. January also expresses similar thoughts: "I obtain self worth through hard work without the help of the government. That is my dream. I want to work hard. I don't need to look at my neighbor and whine about them having more or less."

Jeff and January see the government as just one among several players that has the power to either give out money to a person or to withhold it. Interestingly, the government is perceived to be 'helping out' when it is handing out money, and not just fixing deficiencies in the economic system. They believe that an economic system, without government intervention, is inherently fair to the workers and everyone else involved. How they come to that conclusion, which is a common viewpoint among the more conservative young people in Douglas, is unclear to me. My impression is that the concept comes from television, because their statements often suspiciously sound like catch-phrases that TV commentators on stations such as Fox News make, but I have no further evidence for such a claim.

January and Jeff both have backgrounds from the ideological classes — although one is U.S. American and the other is Mexican. And although their ideas are largely centered around what the government should or should not do regarding the domestic distribution of money, they think and formulate in a generalized way about what government should do — independent of any cultural ramifications.

Conclusion

Class

As we can see, the lifestyles and classes of the informants varies, from the lower white-collar workers such as librarians, and self-employed shop owners such as Garry Mora and Kevin, to those who are clearly members of the lumpenproletariat, who only get day labor occasionally.

This differentiates the community from the communities described by both Ehrenreich (2002) and Whyte (1993). While Whyte describes people who clearly survive as lumpenproletariat under ordered and state-regulated conditions with the occasional store owner showing up, Ehrenreich moves within an environment of total private capitalism in which the informants have no other option than to work and work, without getting anywhere. This option of proletarianization is probably available in some parts of the United States, where there are still jobs left, but in marginal areas such as Douglas, it is no longer a realistic option for the majority.

The Douglasites I meet frequently move between these situations. The opening of a new Wal-Mart brings in new opportunities for those like Maria who try to work hard enough to progress for a few months, but to the lumpenproletariat at the Lerman who have largely given up on employment opportunities, it mainly represents a new source of shopping that has to be considered against their rather fixed spending limits, which are determined by whatever welfare resources they can obtain.

The only observed case of a person actually employing a fairly large number of people occurs in Joe's situation. And this is also not a case of private capitalism, but rather of a struggling self-employed person who has attempted to cut all financial connections with the world around him, but has ended up administrating government money to workers under a state-sponsored program.

Economic constructions of community

However, there is no construction of a localized or national production and consumption circle even though the United States government is a huge factor in terms of the financial situation of many of Douglas' inhabitants. Some Douglasites conduct many local transactions, while others perform more global or national transactions. Neither category leads to a belief that their financial activities are conducted within a closed community.

Therefore, in terms of production, the only community that exists is a world community. However, access to various economic subsidies is not evenly distributed, and the Douglasites seem to realize that.

Chapter 3

Crossing the line

NATIONAL borders are one of the features of our global consumption and production community. And with borders comes the difficulty of 'crossing the line,' which in Douglas is the term used for going across the physical border to Mexico. But there are many other lines that can be crossed, like social boundaries, that divide people into separate groups, cultural boundaries, that separate different 'worlds of meaning' (Donnan and Wilson 1999, 19), and I would add 'language barriers,' that make communication difficult.

Social boundaries can be found everywhere, since they work quite independent of other factors. They simply mean that there are some groups that have more internal than external communication, so that they can be distinguished from the rest of society. These can be very small, like groups of friends, such as the people around El Espejo or around the gun shop. I would expect such groups to exist in any society at any time.

But would one not expect physical borders, language boundaries and cultural barriers to wither away in our globalized world?

During the last few decades, it has commonly been held that the important thing about borders is not what they objectively contain, but how they serve the groups on each side to define themselves in opposition to those on the other side. It is even possible for individuals to permanently cross from one side to the other, and the border will stay intact if those crossing allow themselves to be assimilated into the new culture by accepting its norms (Barth 1982).

However, such an explanation is completely a-historical, because it is to be applicable anywhere and at any time in history without having to take other factors into consideration such as who has power and under what social and structural conditions the crossings happen. In fact, even the anthropological academic community has criticized it for some such deficiencies community in recent years.

However, one needs to look at the historical background of our current level of globalization. If one should name the single most important factor that influenced the current situation in economic terms, it would be the falling of the profit rate[1] particularly in manufacturing, but also in other businesses first in the United States some time between 1965 and 1973 and subsequently worldwide.

Previously Berthoud and Sabelli (1979) had thought the main cause for the current over-production problems was the oil crisis of the 1970's. But as Brenner (2002, 21) points out, the profit rate went from around 25% in the period 1948–69 to around 13% in the period 1979–90 in U.S. manufacturing, and the change already started before the first oil crisis. Nevertheless, in people's memory the oil crisis probably made more of an impact in showing that the politics of the west are not sustainable.

The fall of the profit rate in the manufacturing sector then affected all other sectors as well[2]. The falling of profits due to falling prices has meant that industry needed to regain those profits in some way[3], because no one will invest in a capitalist system if expected returns constantly decrease and one can not be sure to recover the capital on the machines one buys this year three years down the road. Critics such as Neale (2004) point out that that is what most politics in the west have been about since then — although they largely failed so far and profit rates have stayed

---

[1]The profit rate is the amount of return one can expect per invested USD.

[2]Marx (1999, 419–438) tends to attribute the historic tendency of falling profits to technical progress, which leads to higher investments in machinery compared to labor power, and which in turn means that it is increasingly difficult to keep profit rates up given the need to compete in the market.

[3]Tactics to regain profits usually include elements such as decreasing wages or cutting away other side cost such as health insurance for workers

low and with the exception of an economic bubble at the end of the 1990's. One of the important results of these politics was the establishment of various global institutions such as the WTO and IMF, which are to standardize politics around the world and the establishment of global markets for most goods. Another important result was erosion of welfare programs in the west.

The important thing to note is that globalization was started specifically with the goal of weakening workers' power, by making them face tougher foreign competition. Therefore it is not coincidental that physical borders are still present — keeping the exploited from uniting. Therefore, Marxists must have a goal to bring workers and lumpenproletariat together in order to unite their struggle across the divisional lines, and especially across language boundaries and cultural barriers, which are not subject to the same level of elite control as national borders. I hope that the following rather detailed descriptions can contribute towards this precise purpose.

Physical Border

By 'physical border,' I mean the physical border line that can be found on maps and that people have to cross by going through various check points. For those only thinking in materialist terms, this is the only way one can cross a border. And in many ways, this rather simply way of crossing can tell us quite a lot. It is certainly done in many different ways, and people certainly relate different meanings to it. However, the question one needs to ask is "Does this really tell us enough to understand why the border line persists?"

Shopping the hard way

I most frequently cross the border with John. He wants to use me as his Spanish translator, and the fact that I do not really speak Spanish does not bother him much. I pick up enough Spanish along the way in order to ask for his basic needs or relay what he wants to express to the people around him, but there are quite a few mishaps.

John has the idea that everything must be less expensive in Mexico, no matter what the realities are. It is true that some things cost less, but for many items, including certain groceries, Mexicans tend to come to the United States and shop at Food City to get the best prices. When John first approaches me with the idea of buying groceries in Mexico, I tell him this, but he will not let go of his false perception of pricing. After a few days I finally agree to go with him to Mexico. I know where *VH* (the equivalent of K-Mart) is situated in Agua Prieta and we walk there together. On the way, at the border crossing we ask what we can bring back across. We find a customs officer who tells us that anything but chicken and beans should be fine. John wants to walk slowly to look for other stores on the way that might be even less expensive than VH, and also to enjoy the view of the neighborhoods we go through. When we finally arrive, he decides to buy two potatoes and one onion, but he first makes sure to get the VH customer card, so he can get all the discounts possible. He also inquires whether there is a bus back to the border, and so we each purchase a ticket for one dollar. The entire trip for the two potatoes and onion takes us three and a half hours, and when we pass customs, he is asked to surrender the two potatoes because there are restrictions on importing potatoes to the U.S. .

Customs requires me to walk out of the border station and wait for him on the U.S. side. After a few minutes, he comes back without the potatoes. He had offered to eat the potatoes right there and then, but the officer would not allow it.

John also wants to go to a whorehouse in Agua Prieta, but is afraid to ask for where it is. For several weeks we look around the same few blocks in Agua Prieta, and because he does not want me to ask where it is, he never finds out.

The prostitute

One morning, John decides to let the prostitute of the Lerman into his room (see — "Sex life", p. 20). "How are you doing?" I hear her ask him one afternoon while John and I watch TV. "Pretty good, and you? Want some coffee?" he replies and she declines with some

of the only words of English she knows. This is when I deduce that
he has been using her service, since no one else ever talks to her.

John confirms this to me two days later when we are on our
way to Mexico. He wants some penicillin because he is afraid he
may have caught gonorrhea:

JOHN: I told her she could come in and she pulled her skirt
up. It looked like she had been having about 20 lovers in
there and not taken a wash for about a week. I couldn't
take the smell of it. I wanted to throw her back out right
then.
JOHANNES: But then how could you get gonorrhea?
JOHN: Well, I kind of dominated her anyways for a while.
I couldn't get it hard and I just went half way in and
then I pulled it out again. I just kind of wanted to get
it over with. I ended up giving her the ten dollars to
just go away. You know I tried getting it hard but it just
wouldn't.
JOHANNES: And now you think you got gonorrhea?
JOHN: See it has been stinking down there for the last couple of days. [...] I don't want to touch it 'cause it's
disgusting so I haven't washed it yet.

I take John over to the pharmacy that I am familiar with across
the border, since they speak English there. John wants me to ask
for the medicine he needs, even though I let him know that they
speak English, so they find the right medicine, a special penicillin
for gonorrhea treatment. It consists of just four pills that need to be
taken over a period of three days or so.

John looks at the pills for a while and is very critical of them
because they look very small. Then I inquire about the price. "21
dollars!" John almost screams. That is too expensive for four small
pills. "We will be back," John says before we walk on. John wants
to check other prices at other pharmacies. After going to a few that
do not have any penicillin that work for cases of gonorrhea, we go
to one that has a girl in her twenties standing behind the counter;
she obviously impresses John. John does not want me to tell her he
has the gonorrhea problem and not me, so I ask her for the right

penicillin, and when she tells me that she does not have any of that type, I thank her and head for the exit. However, John wants to stay, so he starts looking at an alarm clock on display behind the counter. John tries to communicate with the cashier lady on his own, but she does not understand him at all. He finally gives up before I step into the conversation, and then we leave. Once we are outside, John says that he wants to try just one more pharmacy and if they do not have it, he wants to come back here. "But they didn't have it," I complain. "Just don't tell her it's for gonorrhea," John counters, "them pills they had looked much better and there were 25 in a box." As expected they do not have the correct pills at the next place either, so we return to the pharmacy with the young girl. I ask for the penicillin again, and I just manage to communicate that I also have stomach troubles that I need to treat with penicillin. John grabs the box and pays the 23 dollars, and then feels the need to tell her in English: "You know, he might have contracted some gonorrhea." She realizes the betrayal and tries to get convince us that we did not get the right thing: "No no, está solamente para el estómago." But her protests do not impress John and we hit the exit before she can figure out a more effective strategy to stop either one of us from taking the penicillin.

Zack physical

Zack has much more local knowledge of the border than John. and his consumption pattern in AP is somewhat different, as the following episode will show.

It is a day when John, Angel and I are helping Zack clean his yard (see — "John socializing", p. 99). John and I sit and wait for the others to come back from the recycle station, until we give up and I go back home to sleep.

When I wake up a few hours later, I walk back to Zack's house and all I can see is Angel standing at the car repair shack on the opposite side of the street. He gestures for me to step inside and within a few minutes they have a grill hot and are putting meat of some kind on it. Angel makes sure that I get both a piece of meat and a can of the Food City cola, which I am to learn is frequently consumed by the Lerman crowd. When I have finished my cola,

Angel makes sure that I am offered another one. I refuse but ask him whether he knows where Zack is. I feel somewhat bad for having left him earlier with the entire yard still full of trash.

I walk over to the house in order to check whether he might be in the back yard. I see Zack in the twilight through one of the broken windows. His eyes are wide open and he speaks slowly with a low voice. He tells me he came back and waited for us earlier that day, after he and Angel were finished dumping the trash. I ask him whether he is going to come over and have some meat. He answers that he will be there in a second.

When I go over to his house for a second time, he is gone and has not shown up at the car repair shack. I assume that he has just left with one last truckload so he can return the rented truck, and do not think too much more about it. When I am finished with my cola, I walk back to the Lerman and go to my room.

About half an hour later, I hear the TV turn on outside in the lobby, I walk out and see John sitting on the couch and Mr. Fernandez standing beside the TV. They are discussing their concern that Zack has not come home even though his probation requires him to be home at 6pm every night and it is already 6:30. I suggest that maybe he is just running late with his last truckload. The others agree that that is probably the case, but as time goes on, we get more and more impatient. Mr. Fernandez suggests that the police might have caught him, and we consider calling them. But then we realize that if we ask them it might actually just warn them that he has not returned home. Another discussion we have concerns what we should tell his girlfriend who usually calls at night.

I end up being the one chosen to talk to the girlfriend and so when she calls I explain to her that the money she has wired for the truck earlier that day has arrived, but that Zack now may be in police custody. She is totally crushed and keeps on calling all night for updates.

At about 9pm, Mr. Fernandez suggests to me that I follow him out the back door of the Posada without letting any of the others notice. I follow him to his pickup, we get in and he starts driving. His plan is that he will drive to every club and bar in town, and I will jump out and walk through each one, checking for Zack while Mr. Fernandez sits in the car as close to the front door as possible with the engine running. In one of the bars close to Zack's home, I meet one of the mechanics from the car repair shop. He talks a little about how crazy Angel is, but tells me that he has not seen Zack that night. I am actually not sure that he knows who Zack is at all after having talked to him for a few more minutes. Then I run out, jump in the truck and we are off to the next bar. We never find Zack, but Mr. Fernandez confesses to me that Zack has been talking about "leaving from all of this" — his girlfriend and the probation — the night before.

The next morning at 8:30am, Zack is standing out in the hall talking to Angel. "I'll go to a Spanish speaking church with him now and then I can meet you outside the English speaking church at ten" is his first remark, as if nothing had happened the night before. When I ask him where he has been the previous night, he explains briefly that he had come back at 9pm and gone directly to bed when Mr. Fernandez and I were out looking for him and John was in his room. It is the day when all of us go to church together (see — "Getting to know one another", p. 17).

The Confession

That night I talk to Zack again, and he confesses that he has been out until 3am, drinking and taking drugs across the line. He had actually gone to Mexico twice that day. When I saw him inside his house, he had just come back from his first trip. He circumvented the border controls by telling them that he had forgotten his ID card, so the second time he had to wait until 3am before coming back into the U.S., to avoid the same shift of border guards.

Bruce and The Physical Border

Bruce wants to go to Agua Prieta mainly to go out and experience the night life there. Bruce theorizes that Douglas and Agua Prieta under any "normal circumstances" would be one town. And so limiting oneself only to the Douglas side of the border means just living in a small town that is cut off from most of the world instead of living in a major city. The first thing Bruce points out is that there are sushi bars in Agua Prieta — a good indication of an urban area in his eyes. He tries to set up a meeting with the girls working at La Gardin, who he knows go to dance clubs in Agua Prieta, but that fails because they do not seem interested in taking the two of us along. But he extracts some important information: one cannot just go over there at 9–10pm, when the two of us went over the last time. We have to go cruising until at least midnight or possibly even 1am before we can find interesting nightlife at the clubs.

Bruce, coming from the city of Memphis, Tennessee with a background of what Marx called 'the ideological classes' (Marx 1999, 272)[4], has never tried to go cruising before in his life. I explain the basic principles to him, which I learned while I was an exchange student in a small town in South Carolina a few years back. In his parents' car one night, we try to look cool and gain attention by making a loop, going up and down the main drag and turning around at specified gas stations, as January and her friend Lisa have shown me a few weeks earlier, but I do not know the basic rules of how to be cool, and neither does Bruce. And neither of us finds cruising nearly exciting enough to do it for three or four hours before going to a club in Agua Prieta. So the next time, we decide to skip the cruising part and instead just wait around and then go directly on foot to one of the clubs that one of the girls at the bakery recommended to us. We go there, and check out the scene most of the night without seeing anyone we know. Afterwards, we walk back across the border. The next day, when we enter La Gardin, Bruce is amazed that the staff knows where we were. He asks Michelle a few follow up questions to make sure she is not just conjecturing about a probable course of events, and she is able to answer all his questions. One of the guys driving around town calling me 'Killer Todd' was apparently at the place and remembered what we were doing. "It's like living in a fish bowl," Bruce exclaims later, when telling the story to Todd and Kevin.

The next time we go to Agua Prieta for something major, a few months have passed. Bruce's back is about to break from building the rock dams. Joe gives him time off for a few days, and he comes to Douglas, and wants to go to the doctor. "There is one doctor

---

[4]Government officials, priests, lawyers, etc.

where you pay based on your income," he tells me while we are heading towards downtown Douglas. We find the place, but there is a long wait to get any treatment, so instead he wants to see whether Kevin knows any good doctors in AP that will treat him immediately. Kevin drives us in his Volvo to downtown Douglas, and he gives us the address for a doctor he knows. We drive across the line and at the town square we find the office of the doctor Kevin has recommended. When we enter the office, a man comes out of the door in a business suit, carrying a black suitcase. Bruce explains that it is a representative for a pharmaceutical company. While we sit in the waiting room, there is a woman sitting there with a similar suitcase, and when it is Bruce's turn to enter the doctor's office, there is yet another pharmaceutical representative leaving the office. I wait for Bruce outside and he comes out a few minutes later with a prescription and a letter for Joe saying that he should not work for some time, and a note for Kevin saying that the doctor has a particular drug in his office that Kevin can come by and pick up. The doctor visit costs 20 USD, and the drugs cost 50 USD. "Doctor Feelgood" is what Bruce calls the doctor for the next several weeks, because "he seemed to be willing to write anything I told him to."

After giving the note to Kevin, Bruce asks him who in his family needs the listed drug. "Oh, nobody, but there is always someone who needs it," is Kevin's reply.

When Bruce tells the story to people like Kevin and Todd, he makes a connection between the people from the pharmaceutical company and the price of the drugs, which he judges to be too expensive. He believes that the high frequency of representatives visiting the doctor has influenced him to write many more prescriptions for drugs, and at higher dosage levels.

Winter Visitors

The winter visitors in Douglas are a totally different group of 'real Americans.' This group stays mostly at the RV Park near the golf course. I see some of them every day during the winter months at the library, but most of them stay outside the city unless they need to go to the Laundromat. The Douglas Visitor's Center arranges regular tours for the winter visitors to Agua Prieta, and I sign up for one of them. Joining me on the tour are two Canadian couples in their fifties, a recently divorced woman from Bisbee (the closest town to Douglas) who is on her cell phone constantly, accompanied by her mother and her child. The tour guide is a lady in her forties, who also is an animal rights activist, and the tour bus driver is a young mother in her early twenties.

The guide first shows us a map of Douglas and Agua Prieta and points out how they really join together to constitute a single large city. Then we get on the bus and drive the 200m up to the border. Once across the border, we get out and walk to a shopping place where one can buy sombreros and ponchos. "And the guy who owns the store speaks English," we are assured. The woman from Bisbee looks at some things, while both the Canadian couples buy some ponchos and one of them a sombrero, which they have promised for someone back home. Then we walk another 40m to a small bakery where we are allowed to look into the back room when the actual baking is taking place. I have not been in that particular bakery before, but it is not much different from La Gardin on the American side. The guide buys a little bread, and I do too. None of the others choose to have anything. We get back on the bus and drive another 200m to a pharmacy where they also speak English. We walk to the store next door where they sell piñatas and fillings for them, which we all agree just seem like oversized chips. The bus is not waiting outside when we come back out again, so the guide quickly leads us through the nearby Catholic Church, which happens to be open.

By then the bus returns and after cruising around a bit, we drive to a restaurant that is right on the border, only about 200m from the border crossing. Here we are scheduled to eat a meal. One of the Canadian couples is quick to point out that they have brought their own food. The guide tells them that they still can join us inside, but they make it clear that they prefer to eat their food in the bus. The others come along, but the other Canadians do not dare to eat anything from the restaurant either; instead, they have a drink. The mother from Bisbee and her family have something to eat and so do the guide, the driver and I. The conversation turns towards the subject of languages and their differences and because the guide, the driver and I all know at least two languages, the others, who only speak English, cannot really follow. The Canadian husband says: "I think the only international language is this." He pulls out a 1 USD bill, "if I show this up then everyone will try to get a hold of it no matter what language they speak and I will get what I want."

When we are through with the meal we drive on to look at some maquiladoras from the outside, but we do not stop. We are told that here they produce seat belts and that the workers have a few job benefits such as a cafeteria. I start asking about wages (3 USD per hour) and what kind of labor organization the workers have. The guide seems to know quite a bit of the history of organizing workers in Arizona. But on the matter of organizing workers in Mexico, she explains: "Their unions are different here, [...] here they have government unions." Her answer triggers the Canadians because they can suddenly identify with the questions I have asked, and they start talking about what unions they are in back home. Their sudden agreement with me seems to have to do with the contrast that union-organizing represents, opposed to how U.S. American society is organized, and they have now shown that they are part of "the sane part of the world."

The next stop is the central mall in AP— at the VH. The plan is not to go shopping here, but instead we walk through VH while the guide points out that they offer Corn Flakes, potatoes, tomatoes, tea, and all the other common items that one finds in American stores as well. The others survey most of the shelves, walking up and down in the store, until one of the Canadian men needs to go to the restroom, and we head back out to the bus when he is done.

We drive back across the border and the Canadian couple which has been sitting in the bus finally gets to drink some water once we are back in Douglas, which they are convinced is much cleaner than the water they might have gotten 300m further south.

A few months earlier, I meet a couple at the annual Valentine's Day party that the city arranges for the winter visitors. We are greeted at the golf course country club at the golf course with plastic bags containing various articles from the Douglas Chamber of Commerce: a poster of Douglas, a plastic cup, a few brochures highlighting all the main tourist sites Douglas can offer, etc. . A retiree from Colorado named April greets me at salad bar and invites me to sit with her and her husband, Bill. He is not her first husband and they have only found one another after retiring. She used to be an art teacher, while he used to be a prison guard. "We go to Mexico every year when we come down here," April starts, "I buy colors and frames down there." Whenever they come down to Douglas, they first cross the border in Nogales to stock up on paint and frames for pictures that she paints. According to them, paint is a lot cheaper in Mexico. However, they buy all other items in the United States. When they are in Douglas, they never cross, as it's "very, very dangerous over there." Tonight, April is excited, because she knows that the Mexican dance group from the high school will be performing. Two years ago she took a photo of one of the girls, which she later transformed into a painting. "They are all so cute," April remarks, and tonight she wants to show the painting to the girl. Bill is quite quiet and only seems to ask a few questions in order as to be polite. April has ordered him to take more pictures of the dancers once they come on and he stands up to take a series of pictures while they are performing. April makes sure that she gives the picture to the teacher so she can pass it on to the girl. When the dancers are finished, April and Bill decide to go to bed, and then April offers to have Bill drive me back to town. As soon as April has gone into their trailer, Bill orders me to "buckle up." Now that April is gone, he seems more inclined to talk. In his view, one of the major problems is the huge number of "invaders" who enter the country. "There are many of us," he tries to explain, "that don't like the President's plan [of legalizing certain immigrants] a whole lot."

For the winter visitors, Mexico seems to be a dangerous place. "Douglas is very cheap," I hear several times, and it seems to be the only reason for the winter visitors to come to Douglas. For them, Mexico is only a source for cheap consumer goods and a producer of exotic culture.

Local Youngsters

It is interesting that the Douglas youth cross the border as little as they do. I go across the border up to several times a day, but many of them cross it rarely if at all, even though, it creates considerable difficulty to drink alcohol on the U.S. side of the line. For example, one night Maria and her friends are determined to drink alcohol and we start out by cruising through Douglas, where Maria runs into an old friend a few years older than her. He wants to go party and we agree to pick him up later. First we go cruising a bit more and then we go to 10th Street Park where a few of us eat hot dogs while the others chitchat. It is summer, so Luis and some of the other Cyber teens are at the Park throwing water balloons on cars driving by on 10th street. When we arrive, the police are just about to bust the Cyber teens, so Luis runs over towards us to escape. Then we drive over to Safeway where the three of us who are of legal age go in and buy the alcohol. In the mean time Maria has found out via phone that the friend she met earlier and the guy hosting the drinking party have issues with one another. So instead we decide to go to Harland's house, far outside of Douglas. We drive back to pick up Maria's old friend and then drive out to Harland's house. Once we are there, the girl driving one of the cars needs to go home so now one more person has to get into Maria's car. Brutus is a computer technician for Microsoft in Tucson who has been "out of prison for over a year now."

Once the second car has left, the others realize that Harland does not live there anymore and someone else has moved in. So we head back to town. Maria lets her old friend drive, and he is very drunk. When we hit the highway going into Douglas he almost crashes into the signs and only considerable luck saves us all from being killed. Over his mobile phone Brutus now finds out that he needs to go to his family's home, because tonight is his only chance to meet his cousin. We then drive to the house and drop him off. We cruise for awhile until he is done, and when we return, Maria asks a member of his family, who is connected with the Grand Hotel, whether we can drink in the parking lot behind the hotel. We are given permission but must be very quiet. My thirst for alcohol has lessened considerably after driving for hours on end, so I talk without drinking. We are about 150m from where it would be legal for them all to drink, but instead they take the risk of being caught. "It's private property, the cops can't just come here," Maria explains, "They need a warrant." Bruce doubts that interpretation of the law when I consult him about it later on. It is also getting uncomfortable for the others, so we drive further on to Danny's house instead. Danny lives with his family, but he has his own room and the walls are all full of plastic action figures that have been kept in their boxes. Danny has a video game machine and immediately someone starts up a game of wrestling on it while people are drinking their beers. I think this is a time where I can pass out on the carpet unnoticed, but eventually I am discovered and the combination of my falling asleep and not having anything to drink is what I believe gives me the status of "not the kind of person one takes across the border."

Changing Habits

The border is usually quite open to the kids, but when the drug war breaks out in Agua Prieta (see also — "The drug war", p. 40), most of those who I talk to have an uncle in the family who is involved in drug smuggling and who tells them that "no member of [their] family is safe in Agua Prieta right now." For a period of about three weeks the border is suddenly where the world ends for the youngsters, and they miss going across the line very much, they tell me. John and I still cross to go eat, since we presume that there is no danger as we are not involved in the drug war, but the Cyber teens I talk to seem to think that I am insane for continuing to cross the line. Interestingly, the drug war itself seems to stay on the Mexican side of the border, although there are many guns in the United States and several of the parties involved also seem to have family members on the American side of the border. After a few weeks, everything is back to normal.

Peter's first time

Peter came to Mexico for the first time in 1966. "I feel at home here," Peter tells me, "I have not really been away from Mexico since." However, he always had to work in the United States, because he cannot legally work in Mexico, "unless [he] immigrated," but he does not really have the money to prove that he "wouldn't be a burden on the Mexican government." He has lived many different places in Mexico, because he "just wanted to see the other parts of Mexico," he explains. But he came to Agua Prieta first, and now he has been back for about a year.

When he was discharged from the military, he went back to Texas and married a girl who he had known before the Korean war. After their marriage broke apart, he stayed in Houston for a while. But in Houston, "paper mills stunk and oil refineries stunk," so he thought, "there gotta be some place better than this." So he decided to go back to Douglas. In Douglas he found a taxi driver who he asked, "where all the women are," and he was led to a whorehouse in AP.

He met his second wife at the whorehouse. He convinced her to move to Douglas, and during their nine years of marriage, he managed to stop drinking. But then one day he had a drink with a friend, "and one thing lead to another" and he ended up spending the night in the whorehouse. The next day his wife knew what he had done, and she angrily smoked a cigarette, although she normally never smoked. That day he had to sell some insurance policies in Nogales and pay back some money in Naco, which took longer than he had estimated, and when he came back home, his wife was lying in the bed with a shot through her heart. "She thought I was with some woman again," Peter conjectures. His daughter also died when she and a boyfriend had taken some Angel dust and then had driven their car into a tree. The police had caught the boy a little time earlier, but Peter and his first wife had helped him to stay out of prison.

Peter sees himself as "a case of thrown away life, unfortunately many went with it." He has helped several women who had lived across the border to get settled in the United States. He worries about them now, and he tells me about the case of Irma. She "is not well off at all," but since she is in the U.S., "she is safe," although she is in desperate need of a knee replacement that would cost 45,000 USD, and amount that is completely beyond her means.

Bruce tells me that he meets Bicycle Peter all the time at places like the Mexican Embassy where Peter hunts down copies of birth certificates and such things.

Language Boundary

The language boundary is somewhat harder to cross. That is mainly because one has to have some skill for languages and invest some time into getting familiar with another language. At least to some extent, that is all there is to it.

However, as the first example will show, it is often not only about learning one language, but also about forgetting another.

Oscar, first Hispanic president

Oscar chats with people from Britain a lot, and he invites me for tea several times. His mother does not speak any English at all, but he sees himself as being completely American. He is planning to become President of the United States, "but not during the next two terms." That is why he does not mind if another Democrat wins the current election. Oscar knows all about the official U.S. history in extreme detail. For example, he knows which President was inaugurated where and other similar trivia, and he knows the whole legal process – how laws are drafted and processed through the entire legislative system. He discusses politics extensively with his British friends. In the computer room of the local University of Arizona offices, I witness students asking him about very specific historic details of the U.S. electoral system.

Oscar has some enemies in Douglas, such as Sarah, the librarian. She has issues with him concerning overdue books and a few other matters. Oscar is afraid that this might ruin his chances of becoming President, and when he hears that I have participated in a Dean-for-President campaign targeting all Douglas Democrats and he was not contacted at all, he threatens to leave the Democratic party for good and instead become a presidential candidate for the Republican party. His strategy in any case is to circumvent the necessity of bribery by first earning enough money to pay for the entire campaign — one billion USD. In that way, there will not be any money coming from third parties.

Mr. Fernandez and Zack disapprove of Oscar immediately, because they believe he is gay and "up to no good." Mr. Fernandez might actually know Oscar from an earlier time, but Zack certainly does not. Their disapproval of Oscar is then the basis of their ongoing communication with Oscar. Oscar only speaks English to them, and he sounds just like any other American, while Mr. Fernandez has a distinct Mexican accent, and Zack speaks with a dialect that he himself terms as "ghetto." The first thing Monica tells me about Oscar is that he is almost certainly gay, and secondly that "he doesn't like to speak Spanish." Monica strongly emphasizes the fact that Oscar's mother is completely Mexican when she tells me about it. Oscar's interaction with the community is largely limited to his mother and Art, as well as some of the Cyber teens every now and then. Largely, it seems to be a result of the rumor that he "is gay." It is therefore hardly his fault that he does not have much interaction with anybody except Art at the Lerman. On the other hand, his clear anti-Mexican attitude has probably contributed a lot to the rumors being started in the first place.

Bruce, rock worker

Bruce is fluent in French, and when we walk through the neighborhood while campaigning for Dean, he is able to give basic information to those who do not speak any English at all. Nevertheless, he emphasizes that he cannot speak any Spanish when asked, The first time that he feels that he speaks Spanish well enough is after he has been working with the Mexican workers at Joe's place for a while: "My Spanish is about the dirtiest Spanish ever. I'll probably get my ass kicked if I ever use it anywhere." Bruce is referring to the fact that his knowledge of Spanish is shaped by the class background of those he learned it from, because they use quite crude metaphors related to sexual themes. For example are check dams he and the other workers build are likened to g-strings.

Todd, more than Mexican

Todd is prevented from entering Mexico by court order, so he is restricted to crossing the language boundary and the cultural barrier. When January comes by his house one night when I am not there, and she stays for over an hour. Both independently tell me about the meeting. Todd emphasizes that they spoke Spanish most of the time while January emphasizes the theme of the conversation. When customers who come to El Espejo start speaking English, Todd answers in Spanish when he is confident that they know Spanish. He enjoys telling about the time the Mexican consulate came to the prison he was in, complaining that all movies that were shown were in English, or the time when he was sitting on a bus that was stopped to be checked for illegal immigrants, and he told them he didn't know any English and therefore needed to get all instructions in Spanish. Todd tries to cross the language barrier, and he is quite successful at it.

He sits around La Gardin many mornings for hours and when he sees people whom he knows sitting inside while he is walking by, he enters to talk. At night, when the owners come back for something or another, I often find Todd inside La Gardin talking to the employees. For several months, he is trying to date the 19-year-old Francisca. "She is the daughter of the owner with another woman," Todd explains. She is also the only one who doesn't speak English at all. After Todd loses his job at the environmental project, he asks the owner about getting a job setting up bakery deliveries to different locations within the county. "I'll go down to the prison and they'll easily buy a bunch of boxes," Todd tells me right after he had made a deal to start driving around in one of their trucks. All this shows that Todd actively tries to cross the cultural boundary as well — however, not quite as successfully as he hopes for (see — "Todd crossing without crossing", p. 110).

Cultural Barrier

The third aspect is the crossing of cultural barriers. For some anthropologists (Donnan and Wilson 1999), this is the same as being able to cross the language boundary. Such models seem to simplify what it actually means to be able to speak one language. Sure, if one has perfect and accent-free knowledge of several languages, one can travel to a place where one is known by no one, and act as if one is part of another culture. However, there are other aspects more important than language regarding the way people relate to an individual, which determine if people permit that individual

Photo: Johannes Wilm

Picture 10: Douglas and AP youngsters in an ethnicised show of Mexican culture
— mostly for rich golf tourists?

to become accepted into their culture. For those who want to get
involved in changing the entire world and therefore need to be able
to bridge such cultural gaps, these aspects are of particular interest.

John socializing

Usually when John and I cross the border, we go to a place to eat
and he looks for a new place to buy cigarettes. The first time we go
to Agua Prieta, I take John to a place where I have been many times
and where they have learned to understand my version of Spanish.
We go there for a few weeks about every other day, but then John
wants to go to another restaurant where they barely understand me
and they do not have menus with items I can point at. After a few
weeks, they do understand me there as well, and so John wants to
move on to a third restaurant a few streets further away from the
main road.

No one on the staff understands any English and although
several people are called forth from the kitchen to take my order

either in English or Spanish, no one seems to be able to understand me. John is excited — this is a place he likes! And while all other guests stare at us, he sits down and lets me handle the staff. Finally someone seems to understand my "y él quiere un café sólo" so that also John gets his order. My burrito order is fairly pain-free. When the food finally arrives, there is no coffee for John, but instead he gets a chicken served. "Ah, don't worry. [...] I kind of like this place," is John's reaction, "we need to come here again." The restaurant does not seem to have anything else going for it. The food is what is being served many other places including those that we have been to already, the restaurant itself is somewhat smaller than the previous ones, and we get water from the tap, which according to John "probably contains pee." The only difference is that this place is so foreign that I am not able to give a correct order.

When I tell the story to Kevin, he first says that he needs to tell his wife the story about the chicken for coffee, as she will find it funny. But then he also says "it is good for a person [like John] to be like that [searching the exotic]."

Another way that John tries to cross the cultural boundary might be seen in his taking 'social responsibility' for those he meets in Agua Prieta (see p. 49). Often when we are done with our activities in Agua Prieta, he likes to just sit on one of the benches directly at the border on the Mexican side and look at the cars that go across. For a few weeks John has the idea that he and I should get a car together and drive southward into Mexico. "There we will see the real Mexico — with real poverty," he predicts. John expects that what he sees in Agua Prieta is still one of the most affluent parts of Mexico, and the 'real Mexico' is further down the road. But he never sets forth any concrete plans.

Many of John's attempts of crossing are connected to spending money in Agua Prieta, which lead to no particular lasting bonds or his getting more accepted as a local. But in a way he does cross the cultural boundary, at least towards the Douglasites.

John's first attempts to cross the cultural barriers happen during his first days in Douglas, when he is trying to look for possible friends.

Early on the day Zack disappears (see — "Zack physical", p. 84), John, Angel and I offer to help Zack clean his yard. Zack tells

John and me where it is and we walk over there after visiting the library. Zack wants us to clean the yard first because Zack has rented a truck from a neighbor, which he wants to use to haul the trash away. I know that Zack is not allowed to drive, because he has shown me his identity card — a substitute for a driver license for people that are not allowed to drive — the night before.

We agree to fill a few truck loads that day, and some of the neighbor's kids quickly join us, helping to get the smaller pieces of plastic bags and newspapers that are hanging among the cactus. After a while their parents discover them, and we are left without their help again. Nevertheless, it does not take long and the first truckload is filled. Zack suggests that John and I wait around the yard while he and Angel go to the recycling station. John finds a plastic bowl to sit on, but he offers it to me as he insists he prefers to sit on a stone. That morning John lends me a pair of work gloves, while Angel has to work without any. From then on, I spend more and more time with John and less with Zack, although all of us three hang out together for quite a while.

John and I are sitting on the sidewalk for what seems like several hours. Finally John suggests giving up and in one last attempt to find Angel and Zack, I convince John to walk over to Pan American Highway since we had seen the truck disappear in that direction. John is convinced that the recycling station is the hill we can see in the horizon (which later turns out to be the waste left over by Phelps Dodge), so we give up finding them. I walk home and fall right to sleep, and John also goes home.

While this first attempt of making friends might have failed, during the following months Zack starts calling John "Juan," which he explains to me is the equivalent of John in Spanish. John reacts to his new nickname, but when he is told a few weeks later what it means, he says: "Oh, I thought it was some kind of swear word." When neither Zack nor Angel is anywhere in sight he tells me: "You know, you gotta get along with everybody. Nevertheless, if you don't get along with blacks and Hispanics, you just won't have any friends in prison." I then ask him why he does not try to learn Spanish, and he merely says that if he has not learned it yet, he probably never will.

After John has moved out from the Lerman, he also manages to establish a casual friendship with Marcos, one of the Cyber teens who is said to be especially Mexican by the other Cyber teens. Marcos lives two doors down from him with his family, and John has been invited to watch some football at their place, and when he leaves he gives all his *Sports Illustrated* magazines to Marcos.

"Damn he was a good man," one of the other Cyber teens says openly later during the day that John has left, when I announce that John is no longer in Douglas.

Bruce goes to Tucson

The day that Michael Moore's *Fahrenheit 9/11* comes out, Bruce and I want to go to Tucson to watch it. Unfortunately, Tom has just had an accident the day before, so we cannot take his car. By coincidence I talk to Maria that day, and I find out that she and a few of her friends are going to go to Tucson to look for an apartment and a job for college. I call her up and we agree on meeting on her picking us up the next morning at 6am. "If only you pitch in for the gas, it's going to be fine," Maria says on the phone, "it's only going to be like 4-5 dollars."

The next morning Maria's pickup is waiting outside the Barkers with Maria, Nay and James. First we drive a few blocks to a car wash, because Maria does not "want to drive around Tucson in a dirty truck." "Very Mexican," Todd tells us after we return. It costs Maria 7 dollars. The three others sit in the front and push the seats all the way back so they are practically lying down, while Bruce and I have almost no space. Bruce pulls out a book on the civil war in Rwanda, but Maria turns up the music so loud that I have given up any hope of reading anything. When we later leave the car, Bruce complains: "First they played gangster rap which at least has some kind of style to it, but then they played this utter trash [Insane Clown Posse, etc.]!"

Once we are outside of downtown Douglas, we pull up to a gas station. "I need some money for gas," Maria says loudly so everyone can hear it. I ask her how much, and she says: "30 dollars." Not having much experience with local gas prices, and not knowing who she was referring to, I take a worst case scenario and when Bruce, her, and I are inside the station alone, I ask "Did you mean

30 dollars from each of us or together?" Maria simply answers: "If you wanna do it like that..." but because the bill is only a little more than 30 dollars, Bruce pays it and I am to pay him back later.

We drive on, but as soon as we get to Bisbee, we pull off the main highway again in order to cruise down the main drag. It is barely 7am, and we are cruising slowly down the main drag of Bisbee with the windows rolled down and the music playing at full volume. In the front, our three companions try to look as cool as possible by lying down. In the back, Bruce sits beside me and is reading about how the Hutu killers would cut the heels of the Tutsis who they did not have time to kill before lunch, to prevent them from running away.

Once we are outside of town, the windows are rolled up again, but the music volume stays at the same level. Next we go through a tunnel. As I have learned from a previous trip to Sierra Vista with them, one is supposed to hold one's breath while inside the tunnel. Maria makes a point of hitting the brakes once inside the tunnel until we almost come to a standstill and a car behind us honks at us. As soon as we are in the next town we stop again, this time to shop at a gas station. We stop again at the next town, Benson, which is at the interstate junction, and Maria and Nay walk over to a nearby mall to see if they can get some breakfast, while Bruce and I talk to James. He tells us he just needed to get out of Douglas for a while, and really is not sure about the plan of finding a common apartment in Tucson that Maria had mentioned.

The last stop is right before Tucson. We are already within the city limits, when Maria pulls off the road again.

MARIA: If you wanna gas up one last time, it's only going to be like 20 to 25 dollars.

BRUCE: [*Very aggravated*] Why do you ask us? We paid thirty dollars already!

MARIA: Well didn't you say that you wanted to pay 30 dollars each?

JOHANNES: That was asking, not proposing.

MARIA: [*seemingly taking it lightly*] Oh OK, well I'm going to pull off anyways. Are you sure you don't want to gas up?

JOHANNES + BRUCE: No [*The truck stops and Maria, Frank and Nay run inside to buy candy. Bruce and Johannes stay at the car.*]

JOHANNES: Maybe it's a cultural thing.

BRUCE: [*mockingly*] A 'cultural thing'! It's a rip-off; that is what it is. The tank is 3/4 filled and so they already got us to pay for them to go both ways and they got enough gas to go cruising around Tucson as well!

We drive into Tucson and Maria drops us off at Robert's apartment. Bruce tells him the story of our journey. Bruce emphasizes the amount we had to pay, the music that was played, the seating arrangement, the car wash, and the amount of time the trip took as a result of the frequent stops. Robert decides to call Sarah and tell her about it: "Mom needs to fire her." Sarah later says: "I didn't tell Robert the other day that I'm not going to act upon it, as it's not library related. But she sure must be losing friends fast doing that." When I tell Kevin the story, he says: "I could understand that you wouldn't quite know what is acceptable, but I don't get why Bruce let them exploit him like that."

Peter living in the United States

During the first few months that I am in Douglas, Peter continues to live in Agua Prieta. He crosses the border at least once a day on his bike and one can frequently see him riding around Douglas, where he stops at El Espejo, the library, and occasionally Wal-Mart. After we schedule his first two interviews, we meet at the border and ride across to his house, which is about 9 blocks from the borderline. "He is paying way too much for that big house," Todd believes, but Peter wants to keep it for when his "future wife" moves to Agua Prieta (see — "Bicycle Peter", p. 206). The house has a living room and a separate sleeping room in which he has prepared a double bed for him and his wife, and a children's bed, which is just a mattress that is lying on the floor. There is also a chair equipped with special head and arm latches. "My future wife likes to be restrained," he explains.

The rent, combined with frequent payments to his fiancé, is too high for his "monthly checks" though. He tells me he has made a deal with the landlady, who allows him start paying the rent the next month, but then she reconsiders and suddenly decides that she needs the rent earlier, and she gives him two dates by which two installments must be paid. Peter knows that he cannot make the second installment, but agrees anyway. The lady also owns a grocery store close by that usually has given Peter credit until his check has come in. But once the landlady has informed him of the two installment dates, no further credit is available to him. That is when Peter resorts to eating cookies at the library.

After a few weeks Peter is thrown out of his house, so he keeps on looking for another place all around AP. When he finally finds one where both the amount of rent and size is right, he is quite excited. A few days later though, they tell him they do not want to rent it out to him. "Peter, they say you live like a swine," is what the lady in charge gives him as a reason. Peter is sure that his former landlady has spread rumors about him around all of Agua Prieta. The third time I meet Peter at his home, he has moved to a trailer park that is twenty minutes by bike north of Douglas. He had a debt with the landlord there, but he has agreed to let him stay on condition that Peter helps some. "But now I suddenly have to clean all the trailers around here," Peter feels cheated, "when they are empty, that is."

The first two times when I meet with Peter at a scheduled time, it is at the border station. The last time it is at his trailer. I make sure to show up ahead of time the first two times, and he, being slightly late, comments on it the second time: "Wow, I have never met a person who was on time like that." The third time, I leave Douglas about half an hour prior to the scheduled meeting, but since I am only following a loose description Peter has given me on the previous day at El Espejo, I end up getting lost and am about half an hour late. Peter does not seem to mind, but while I start making excuses for my delay, Peter comments: "Well, you're on Mexican time."

Similarly, when I consider conducting an interview with Jeff, I tell him about my problem of being unable to schedule many meetings, as people tend to forget about them. Jeff understands, and tells me: "Well, to Hispanics, schedules are more of an abstract idea than actual, concrete thing. And I'm sure they would admit it." So in that sense, Peter certainly has gotten some of the cultural codes right.

The trailer park

Upon returning to Douglas the second time, I try to find Peter, because I assume that he must have moved. Surprisingly, he still lives at the trailer park, although in a smaller trailer. Two ladies, Rosa and Carolina, both friends of Maria's, are also living at the same trailer park. Also living there is a friend of Kevin's — Roger Below, a Polish Jew who had been in Douglas and has recently come back after staying in San Diego for several years. The first time I ride my bike out there to meet both Peter and Roger, only Peter is home.

Rosa

The night before I plan to visit Peter and Roger again, Maria invites me to drink with Nay, her sister Robin, and Rosa one night. Rosa appears to be in her late forties or early fifties, and she has four kids, several of which still live with her. She is not from Douglas and has been living all over the country. Robin and Nay are with us, and we sit in Rosa's living room drinking some hard liquor with just enough soda to hide the awful taste of the nearly pure alcohol. One of the kids wakes up when we arrive and Rosa charges him:

> Oh no! [addressing the girls] Do you guys have some
> kind of magnet that makes him wake when you come?

The kid says very little and cuddles up on the sofa. Also there is a dog and Maria has brought a house for it.

ROSA: Now is that one of them kinds that gets cold when it's
warm and warms him up when it's cold?
[*The doghouse that Maria brought is made out of pure plastic.*]
MARIA: Yeah, exactly.

The rest of the night we sit on the couches in Rosa's trailer drinking and talking while the dog runs around. Robin tells us she has entered a program that allows her to stay in Florida for half a year and earn college credits by working at Disney World. Rosa is upset that the program is "anti-union."

ROSA: Now they have unions there [...] and then they go around to the colleges and take in these kids [who are not unionized] [...]
[*Rosa turns towards Robin*]
ROSA: Now you have to think a bit when they come there to the college and tell you about all this great stuff.
[*Robin turns her head away for a few seconds and does not answer.*]

Later on Rosa complains about the high amount of Mexican influence in Douglas: "Now him here needed to get a book on American football [pointing at the boy who now sleeps besides her]. Do you think they have any of that at the library? Of course not! Foosball — that's what they have." Rosa does not like Douglas and she thinks it is one of the worst places in the U.S. and tells us in detail just how horrible it is. The girls seem to take her half seriously. I also know Maria has started talking about the situation that they all have in common — that they are "stuck in this town."

Peter

The next day I want to visit Peter and Roger during the daytime. First I go to Peter's place, but I do not mention that I have met Rosa the night before. Towards the end of my visit, Peter starts complaining about the new managers of the trailer park:

PETER: Now they are not taking care of the place. Things don't get fixed, and they don't check on the people who come here.
JOHANNES: What do you mean by 'checking on people'?
PETER: Two pieces of ID and calling in to see if the car is stolen. [...] Now what you have coming in here is all kinds of white trash.

It is quite clear that Peter is thinking of Rosa, who lives almost right across from him. In turn, when I come by a few days later and meet Rosa and Maria at the entrance, Rosa reacts when she hears I am also to visit Peter: "Uh, Peter? [...] He is a known child molester, registered and everything."[5] Peter is happy that day, since he has had sex with one of his Mexican women the night before:

> She came over here to visit me and we listened to some old music. [...] and we were sitting close on that couch right here. Then after sitting there for a while she said: 'Peter, you haven't shown me your house yet' and I said: 'oh sure, come along.'
>
> [They go into the bedroom and sit down on the bed]
>
> And then she said: 'Peter, now you're too old and I'm too fat.' 'Oh no, you're not too fat, we can make this happen, we just need some oil'

And he goes on to explain how he looked around the whole trailer trying to find oil and how he first came back to her with the bicycle oil, before they finally used the vegetable oil. "I slid off the first times — right into the wall!" Peter continues. He then secured the covers of the bed with duct tape that is now covering most of the bed when I inspect it.

Roger

Roger is not home the first time I come to visit him, and although I come back several times, I never meet him there. Instead I meet him at the library a few times, and once we visit Kevin together. Roger knows Kevin from an earlier time that he lived in Douglas. Back then he was looking for meteorites out in the desert as he believed there would be great business in meteorites. "I even found one," he explains, "but I just never got to sell it." Now Roger is looking for shrapnel from World War One instead. "I got the idea

---

[5]By checking the Internet that night, I find out that he is not registered as a child molester.

of putting them together when they got that new glue at Wal-Mart," he explains.

According to Kevin, a black drug dealer killed Roger's son, so he has never been too happy about blacks. But since he returned from San Diego, he has also become quite anti-Mexican. Allegedly, they "trash the neighborhood once they move in," he tells me about his experience in San Diego. Roger complains a bit about a group of Mexicans at the trailer park that is playing music loud at night, but when I probe further he is not extremely negative, but he still shows some discontent for the non-whites. Roger shows another perspective when he and I visit Kevin in Mexico, and says that what Mexico needs right now is a "real strong revolution" to overthrow the landed classes.

Rosa and Peter both respect Roger quite highly, and both only speak kindly of him. Peter has not understood Roger's discontent with Mexicans, and perhaps neither has Rosa. However, Roger is not quite as positive toward his fellow trailer park inhabitants, and does not spend much time with them.

Analysis

What is interesting about the trailer park scene is that the conflict lines follow ethnic divisions, even though all the characters involved are Anglos. The question of class also comes in to play. They all have about the same amount money, but nevertheless Peter sees Rosa as "white trash." The classification here is made based on the understanding or the lack of understanding of Mexican culture.

For Rosa, both class and class struggle seem important, and a large part of the Douglas population wants to break unions, in her view. It is likely that her distaste of Mexican culture is connected precisely to the fact that Mexico represents an excess of labor power that seems to be threatening U.S. unions.

The class issue shows up in a different way in the case of Roger. Although his anti-Mexican sentiment seems to be based on a culturalist understanding of the world, he cannot stop thinking in class terms when he talks about the necessity of a revolution in Mexico.

Art & Tom

Although Art and Tom do not interact very much, they have in common that they both seem to have the idea of crossing the border in an abstract way, without being able to cross the actual cultural boundaries.

Tom and Sarah had a satellite dish to watch American TV. But some time before I arrive they have chosen to throw it out. Tom explains: "We realized, we were watching movies every single night." But that does not mean that Tom has stopped watching TV. Now he only watches Mexican TV, and although he really does not know any Spanish, the TV seems to be on just about every night. "I guess he would like to be Mexican," as Bruce explains. At the same time, Tom does not have much respect for Mexican cultural codes. When he and Sarah go to a Catholic Mass attended primarily by Mexicans, he wears "his finest 'Buffy the Vampire Slayer' t-shirt," as Sarah mockingly describes later on.

Tom's problematic relationship with his surroundings becomes clear when he has an accident with his new truck. He is driving in downtown Douglas one Friday, when a Hispanic woman who speaks only Spanish hits him from the side. He tells me that after the accident the place was quickly filled with lots of people, but they were all just concerned with her. "I felt my feelings were not really respected," he explains on the following Sunday. For the entire weekend he cannot see the police report. He is afraid that the people helping the lady, whom he believes clearly was at fault, might have given a description of the accident blaming him instead. It is only on Monday that he finds out that the woman's report matched his own account of the accident.

Art only crosses the border one single time when John and I ask him to. It is during the time when he still lives in his car, and when we are on the other side, Art announces: "I am now as far away from my car as I have been in months." We have a burrito and drink one beer at a restaurant that John and I are going to go to repeatedly from now on. But after the first beer, Art's budget constraints kick in, and I also decide not to have another. Instead, we start walking around, looking for John's whorehouse. We happen to walk by the library, and Art is adamant that we should go in. Once we are inside, the one employee starts speaking to us in Spanish. Art completely ignores the Spanish and starts telling him in fast English that as they have a foreigner with them (me) and because he likes libraries, he just needs to look around. The employee does not understand anything he says, but lets us look through the collection. A few days later, Art talks about how poor Mexico is. He exemplifies that by the way the library looked, and by the fact that it had no Internet connection.

Although Art does not have the skill to cross language barrier nor the cultural flexibility to cross the cultural boundary, he has his idea of opening borders from a technical perspective. Art has been reading and studying a lot about general aviation, and he thinks that soon everybody will have single-person flying wing that can land and take off like a helicopter, which will take a person anywhere, once the person inserts the coordinates of the destination. Country borders will therefore be bypassed by the third (vertical) dimension, and it will be impossible to maintain border security. "When people can vote with their feet," Art is sure, "that is going to be real democracy!"

Todd crossing without crossing

Although Todd manages to cross the language boundary as described, he never manages to get into a relationship with the 19-year old, and the family seems to mock him for his idea of trying to date her. Several times she comes over and talks about going to a dance hall in Agua Prieta, where Todd cannot go due to his parole. Nevertheless, he gets fully dressed up and waits for her at least one night after she has said she will meet him to go out. She never comes, and when I mention to one of the employees at La Gardin the next day that he was waiting, she thinks I am joking. One time when I am at El Espejo with Bruce, the same employee asks whether Todd and Kevin are actually preparing the food at El Espejo. When Bruce and I confirm this assertion, she asks: "Why don't they just put a girl there to make the food? I wouldn't trust eating something Todd has made." And also the job that Todd has been promised at La Gardin never materializes. The morning that he is to start, he has showered and put on clean clothing only to

Photo: Johannes Wilm

Picture 11: The rock working crew only speaks Spanish. Todd is the exception.

hear that they must review the legal issues first. Another date is set, and again that morning they tell him that he cannot start quite yet. This continues for months and every time there is something in the way. I am the first to suggest that they might just be looking for excuses to put him off, but for a long time he is confident that he will eventually get the job. Apparently, Todd is not permitted to cross the cultural boundary when he tries to.

Nevertheless, he earns the respect of the bakery family in other ways. When I first move in with Todd, he is leaving for Joe's on the same day and Art and John wish to make food at Todd's place. For them it is a way to get away from the others at the Lerman. John in particular has turned somewhat suspicious of both Angel and Zack at the time. We plan to make food inside the house and eat it on the parking lot between Todd's house and the bakery. Art makes the food and John fetches 12 cans of beer at Circle-K. While they are performing those tasks, the bakery girls come over and talk just to Art for a little while to find out who he is. It is only when Todd comes back the next weekend that Francisca complains to him that

I did not "respect his property" by inviting others over like that.

Another time, Todd stops coming to the bakery for a few days, and so Michelle starts worrying whether he might feel insulted by something they have said. At the time, I believe that is the case, so I confirm her suspicion. A few hours later I come back at La Gardin, and by now she has found out that he has not been showing up lately, because he has been busy on some of his other projects. So just like Peter, he is also included — at least in a limited sense.

Jeff staying where he is

Jeff is one of the few Anglo kids I meet, and my first impression is that he is not trying to cross the language barrier, because he tells me he does not know Spanish. However, when I interview him, the reason behind this is revealed to be more complex. He actually did take eight years of Spanish classes in school, "but they don't teach the basics. [...] And it's not a problem; if I needed to understand something my dad and my friends all know it." Jeff remembers his earlier years in school when people tried to tell him that Spanish was the language to know: "People would say: 'here we speak Spanish' [...] many thought it was like this everywhere; that it was odd to be white anywhere."

Maybe as a result, Jeff is not in complete agreement with many Douglas teenagers, even today. In a mail, he describes them:

> OK, most girls, or boys, know nothing of politics in Douglas. Other than they hate Bush for reasons unknown to them. But it's "cool."
>
> [...]
>
> But these kids don't truly believe in anything, except what they like to see themselves believing in.
>
> It's like only looking in the mirror that makes you look the most attractive. Its image than music second. Image with no substance. So these kids grow up not even knowing who they really would be, had they not molested their own minds with what they wanted to want.

Jeff also tells me during one of our first meetings that before he got together with January, he used to mock her group for going across the line to party at the clubs. The first time he goes clubbing in Agua Prieta is during graduation, and "it was awful," as he tells me later.

Kevin, the borderless

Kevin crosses the border all the time, as he is living on the Mexican side and works on the American side, but I never actually see him cross before my second visit to Douglas. But the facts that he has been building up a small network of Mexican juice bars and his wife is Mexican show he has been able to also cross the cultural boundary. His contact network reaches far in all directions and it is said he is able to get people released from Mexican prisons within minutes, no matter wherever they are in Mexico. About his wife, he says: "You know I don't want her to go out and work like all the others." He does not want a "normal American life" that consists of both adults working all the time, while leaving the children at home alone.

Kevin is mainly frustrated with Mexicans who "deny their Mexican heritage." One example he frequently talks about is his neighbor who is from Mexico, pointing out that he has not been in Mexico for the past twenty years. "He says he has no business going there," Kevin explains, "if I would tell some of those people something like that Mexico has a bus system that works better then it does in the U.S., they'd say: 'Bullshit!' just because they don't know."

The emphasis on the Mexican and Spanish culture can be seen in Kevin nearly all the time. One time, when January and Carolina wish to ask Todd about conditions for renting his house, I take them to El Espejo. They introduce themselves as January and Carolina with an English pronunciation and Kevin greets them while repeating their names using a Spanish pronunciation. After we have left, the girls talk about his greeting:

JANUARY: Did you notice he corrected our names to Mexican?

CAROLINA: Yeah it made me feel kind of ... [incomprehensible]

Conclusion

As we can see, there are different difficulties connected to crossing the various lines.

However, two examples stand out:

Bruce manages to speak Spanish and go to Mexico, but it does not lead to him understanding the Douglas youth any better. Although the Douglas youth generally does not see itself as Mexican, the fact that clearly distinguishes them from youth in the rest of the United States is that they understand some the cultural codes and the language of Mexico, at least to the extent that the amount of their understanding creates a separate cultural domain that Bruce cannot penetrate. This domain is not distinguished by language in quite the same way as that of "real" Mexicans, because most of their communication is conducted in English, and all the music they listen to is American.

For example, during our the trip to Tucson with Maria, Bruce prefers to read books as he wishes to kill time and to shorten the trip to be as efficient as possible, while Maria and her friends see the trip itself as something to be extended and enjoyed to the fullest. The fact that they dare to overcharge us for the trip probably comes from this fact: Bruce and I neither conform to their ideas of 'coolness,' nor do we seem to progress towards that goal. That might be why Maria is unsure about what are permissible actions within the cultural boundaries in the conversation with us.

But then there are those like John, whose knowledge of Spanish and Mexican culture is on a much lower level. At first sight, it appears that he cannot hope to be included into Mexican culture at all, so he chooses a different path. While John sees himself as being discriminated against because he is Anglo in Douglas, in Mexico he wants to experience the most exotic situations possible. It is not important for him whether or not he can communicate with people, but rather it appears at first that he wants communications to be broken down as much as possible. John crosses the border to Mexico in order to cross into the mystique and exotic. His lack of knowledge of the local culture and Spanish means that he will always keep a certain distance, and so it keeps its mysticism.

Although he needs to express enough to get by, he does not want my Spanish to get good enough to end all ambiguities.

At the same time, he seems to have some more common understanding with many those Mexico-affiliated Douglasites he contacts, seemingly more than Bruce. Probably part of the difference can be accounted for by their educational background and the 'habitus' formed by it[6]. Another part is though to what degree one is accepting not only of the 'foreign' but also of the 'non-logical' behavior of others. Although Bruce is politically more liberal than John, John is more accepting of people behaving in ways that do not seem for him to make sense.

Ideas about Mexico

All those who have stopped looking for work, regardless of actual income, see Mexico primarily as a producer of consumer goods; John, representing the lower end of the income scale, and the winter visitors, representing a higher level on the income scale, seem to cross the border for the sole purpose of purchasing consumer goods. The high school kids, Bicycle Peter, Kevin, and Bruce cross the border for other reasons as well. Seemingly, the purpose of crossing the border is independent of the means of how one gets across. The high school kids and winter visitors drive their cars, John and Bruce walk, and Bicycle Peter rides his bike. It also seems to be independent of the number of times that one crosses: Bicycle Peter, John and Kevin cross up to several times a day, while everyone else crosses less frequently. The key to what people cross for seems to be their conceptual model of Mexico including more than just a place to shop.

Historical Aspects

Had I been in Douglas during the 'good old days' of high profit American capitalism, while Phelps Dodge was still operating there, Douglasites would have been strictly segregated according to race in the earlier period, or according to income levels in the latter

---

[6]'Habitus' designates embodied aspects of culture that one has to be socialized into as a child (Bourdieu 1987).

period. Bruce, Art and Tom, all with somewhat more of an intellectual background also find themselves in this classless society in which everyone is part of the lumpenproletariat. And although all of them partially see their own situation as being a result of their own choices, these choices have been severely limited by the crisis of capitalism. In a situation with more public employment opportunities paid for by higher levels of taxes, class stratification would occur, and they would create an intellectual elite with commensurate jobs.

Material Reasons for Persistence of the Border

If we are to look at the continued existence of the border given the historical situation, we might be surprised that it has not dissolved more. With the large population of lumpenproletariat and no bright future for anyone on either side of the border, why do people still differentiate between Mexican and American?

Let us look at two possible tendencies that Marx sees nationalism moving towards: either disappearing due to overwhelming mixing across national boundaries, or strengthening due to its effect of obscuring class interests and replacing them with imagined "national interests," which are portrayed as being common interests held by all members of the nation, but in fact are interests held by the ruling elite of society (see also p. 212). Which of these tendencies can we observe in Douglas?

The winter visitors could discover the exact same products in the Mexican VH that they are familiar with at home. This falls in line with Marx's first interpretation of the position of the national aspect of states as losing more and more of the features that set them apart from other nation-states.

At the same time, they perceived, wanted to perceive, or pretended to perceive Agua Prieta as a very different and exotic place. The two paradigms do not seem to be contradictory, but rather complementary in practice. The cultural barrier can therefore persist despite changing material circumstances.

Particular features

And also, one should not forget the particular features of this specific border. Although capitalism clearly has transcended the border, and the 'universal interdependence' between the involved capitalist countries is slowly becoming a reality, the two involved countries are not equally developed and huge differences continue to exist. As the radical dependency theorist Andre Gunder Frank (1975) points out, capitalism works with various zones, some central and other peripheral, of which all are equally essential for world capitalism; the 'underdevelopment' of Mexico is a direct product of the over-development in the United States. The reason has to be found historically in the period of colonization of the Americas, when all but the area of the United States and Canada had an organized labor force and raw materials that could be exploited and therefore started out as areas exploited by elites of key western cities, and they have siphoned off a certain surplus value to these western elites ever since (Frank 1975, 441–442). In contrast, the U.S. North-West profits on foreign trade in manufacturing and gradually built itself up as a regional superpower and later as a world superpower (Frank 1975, 451–456). In order to do that, it had to put other areas under its control, and this included Mexico, among others.

But also the underdeveloped areas can be differentiated. Frank compares areas that have had little contact with the West for some time, due either to temporary crisis in the West or to general inaccessibility, with those that recently have had contact with the West. His findings are that instead of becoming more westernized by having contact with the West, the areas that have had contact with the West and have been subsequently dropped due to changes in the world trade pattern, are some of the most underdeveloped and archaic areas that exist, while those areas that have been isolated for a while have been much more likely to develop (Frank 1995). This would give an economic explanation for the underdevelopment of Agua Prieta. The small-scale study of anthropological fieldwork cannot of course document all these features through observations, but that does not mean that they do not have an influence on the relations that the fieldworker observes.

In Agua Prieta, there are a number of maquiladora factories placed throughout the town that are foreign-owned, and Wal-Mart and Food City are both strategically building strategies on attracting Mexican customers. The opposite of John's shopping is a very common phenomenon, and there are always dozens of shopping wagons standing at the pedestrians' entrance to Mexico buying manufactured goods. A surplus value is extracted from Agua Prieta both through employment and through the sale of Asian mass-produced commodities — mainly to centers in the U.S. . In the sense that they are also seen as a market for consumer goods, they do not fit quite into the scheme used by many of the main proponents of dependency theory. One of these is Samir Amin who explains that one of the main differences between salaries paid in the West and those paid in the third world is that those paid in the West are seen by the capitalist not only as an expense, but also as a market for the sale of mass produced goods, while wages paid in the third world are seen only as an expense, because they produce exclusively for export or luxury goods for their own elites (Amin 1984, 204–208).

Now, in the next three chapters we will look at how Douglas relates to the United States and determine whether Douglasites are mainly exploiters or if they are being exploited.

Chapter 4

Crime

P ART of a global exchange network or not, there are some things that are particular to Douglas and which create an understanding of a local community. The key defining theme for Douglas is probably the amount of corruption and other crimes people connect with the city. Although corruption and crime can be found in many other towns, but what sets Douglas apart is that for many Douglasites, it is a part of their self-definition.

On a normative level, most Marxists look at criminal behavior as a result of the laws of any given country primarily reflecting the interest of the bourgeoisie, because this class controls society and therefore can shape the laws (Marx 1999, 331). Crime that is conducted in order to gain a fairer share of what is produced by either members of the proletariat or the lumpenproletariat is therefore legitimate.

But does this apply to the types of crime I have seen in Douglas? We have already looked at some economic crime but there are also those crimes that are not inherently economic in nature or at least have aspects to them that extend beyond merely the economic sphere.

The Structuralist View

On an analytical level, one common thing for Marxists to look at is the structure of society when trying to explain various things. In

Picture 12: Prisoners working on Douglas downtown roads

the case of crime, it is much about the idea that crime has to be seen in a larger social context, which is mainly shaped by productive relations (Colvin and Pauly 1983, 513). The orientation a person has towards authority is heavily determined by the person's class background as compliance structures at workplaces differ between white collar and blue-collar workers. Peer groups among youth largely mirror their parents' class background, and they operate with differing levels of coerciveness (Colvin and Pauly 1983, 514– 516). Further, capitalism induces economic crises, when a labor surplus is created as a result of newer, more efficient machinery.

Many also make a distinction between those workers who have worked in the monopoly sector, which controls mostly through extensive management structure, and those working in the competitive sector, in which control is given by control structures that swing unpredictably (Colvin and Pauly 1983, 534–536). Parents who work in the competitive sector do therefore tend to punish their children equally unpredictably, and the children do not ever learn of any consistency in their parents' behavior and therefore develop a moral code that it is okay to break the law if one can get away with it (Colvin and Pauly 1983, 536).

The Political-Economical View

Another common way of looking at crime from a Marxist perspective is to try to explain why capitalist societies create a desire for criminal behavior:

On one hand capitalism depends on building up a desire for material goods beyond what is needed for pure survival in order for people to perform alienating, meaningless and unrewarding tasks, and on the other hand it includes the constant production of an excess population, or a lumpenproletariat, that is restrained from fulfilling these desires. (Chambliss 1975, 149–150)

Another contradiction lies in the fact that the ruling class controls both the means of production and the state, and this inevitably leads to criminalization of the working class. This is because part of the repertoire of the ruling class in the class struggle is to design the laws to follow their own interests, and partially this is done by defining behavior that might strengthen the working class as criminal (Chambliss 1975, 150–151).

Marx says that the existence of crime actually has a positive aspect, because it diminishes competition in the working class to a certain extent because it not only provides the criminal with a higher living standard, but also offers another segment of the working class with jobs in law enforcement (Chambliss 1975, 151).

Altogether then, crime has four basic features:

1. Behavior is defined as criminal because it is in the interest of the ruling class to do so.

2. The law is enforced against the working class, but not against the ruling class.

3. Industrialization leads to an extension of criminal law to force laborers into submission.

4. Crime is only crime insofar as it is defined as such.

Further, crime will have two main consequences:

1. It reduces the lumpenproletariat by providing jobs in law enforcement.

2. It diverts the working classes' attention from exploitation.

Crime in borderlands

Generally, in borderlands there are three major types of crime: those connected to illegal migration, those connected to prostitution, and those connected to smuggling. In addition, partially as a result of the above, tax evasion is also a common phenomenon (Donnan and Wilson 1999, 88). All of these can be found in Douglas as well, but there are many other crimes to be found in Douglas, as we will see in the following examples.

The close proximity of the border probably has a lot to do with the special status that the law has in Douglas, but that does not fully explain the situation. In Miller's account of his trip along the entire border in the early eighties, Douglas is almost entirely defined through the strong anti-immigrant feelings that some of the Anglos in the town hold. The Douglas as it can be experienced in 2004 and 2005 has a lot in common with Miller's description of Starr County, Texas, which is described as defining "smuggling [as] a way of life" (Miller 2000, 27). Lou, who works at the Douglas Wendt house, almost exactly mirrors Miller's description of this county in his description of Douglas, with pizza delivery boys flaunting the hottest car brands, when he describes the youngsters in Douglas. Due to the embarrassment that some members of the 'cultural elite' feel about the rampant crime, they try to gloss over it by finding things that are more 'positive' and emphasizing them. This is a common strategy in Douglas as well.

The people of Starr County were mostly unemployed during Miller's trip, while Douglas still had Phelps Dodge to keep the economy going at that time. It therefore seems to be the increase in unemployment that has been one of the deciding factors that turned Douglas into what it is today.

Now let us look at some of those crimes and see to what extent the traditional Marxist models help our understanding.

John's got a gun

One Sunday afternoon, when I am getting back from Mexico with John, he offers to let me take a shower at his place. John has been making this offer almost every day after I have moved out of the Lerman because Todd does not have any hot water, so I think nothing of it. We pass Todd's house and I drop my backpack off and get my shower gel and towel and then we continue on walking to his place. On the way, John starts talking:

JOHN: You know, when you talk to Art the next time could you ask him whether he still has his gun?

JOHANNES: Sure ...

JOHN: But, you know, don't tell him I asked. Just say you have a friend who wants to go hunting with it.

JOHANNES: OK?

JOHN: I just want to know whether he still has it, you know, that's all.

JOHANNES: ?

JOHN: Well see, I saw a gun in the trash can the other day ...and it looked kind of like a rifle.[*I Believe* JOHN *is aware that Art's gun is a rifle*]

JOHANNES: In the trashcan? Like deep inside of it?

JOHN: No it was just lying there on top of it. It wasn't even covered. The barrel was even sticking out; that's how I saw it.

JOHANNES: So is it still there?

JOHN: Ehm, no see, I took it. Imagine what Marcos and some of his friends had done if they found it... You know they go and smoke some dope and then they start playing with it and then suddenly they put somebody's eye out.

JOHANNES: So where is it now then?

JOHN: I cleaned it and put it under my sofa.

JOHANNES: OK?

JOHN: But, you know, it probably doesn't even work. It was rusty and all. I probably couldn't even shoot anything with it.

JOHANNES: Well, but it's still dangerous.

JOHN: See, I don't even have any clip for it; the clip is missing. I just want you to look at it.

[*We arrive at his apartment, and not being quite sure what I'm going to await, I follow him to the sofa. He moves the sofa and shows me this shooting weapon, which I am unable to classify but which is about a meter long. John wants me to hold it and I do for a second before I give it back.*]

JOHANNES: Hmm OK, so you don't think it works, huh?

JOHN: Nah, it might, you know. But I don't know whether it would do much good.

JOHANNES: For what? What do you want to do with it?

JOHN: I'm probably not going to use it...but you know, I might.

JOHANNES: But are you supposed to have any guns at all? I mean since you are a convicted felon and all?

JOHN: Ah, I don't think they care. See and if they come here to take it, I might just shoot them. ...You know, I might just have to shoot them all. You know, all them crooks. And you know them cops are crooks around here as well...It's the water. It tastes like shit; like somebody peed in it. I might just need to straighten that up...

JOHANNES: Don't you think that is just going to put you into even deeper trouble? ...Why don't you give the gun to me and I'll put it in my back pack and get it out of here and I'll promise I won't tell them where I got it from. ...But it's your decision, you know that.

JOHN: Well, you know, they might just use it to shoot me then. You know they are looking for guns all the time themselves. They might just be happy that you give them a free one like that.

JOHANNES: Well it's your decision, and I'm not going to tell no matter what you choose to do.

JOHN: You got scared, huh?

JOHANNES: Well, a little...

JOHN: Go ahead; I'm not going to shoot you while you are taking your shower.

JOHANNES: Well, thank you.

After the quickest shower in my life, John is standing in the kitchen. I apologize and tell him I have a very important date with Todd at his house right then before I run to the door.

After a bit of running around, I get a hold of Bruce, and he comes downtown. Todd and Art sit outside Todd's house, and they continue to do so, even after hearing that John might be up to no good.

Bruce takes the situation somewhat more seriously, and he suggests that we go over to the "pig station" (as Todd calls it) and file a report. "Your concept of being an independent researcher will be smashed all to pieces then though," Bruce argues, but he also agrees that I should report on it nevertheless. Before we drive over to the former railway station, which has been given a new purpose, we drive by John's apartment in order to be absolutely sure what the address is. When I get to what looks like the former ticket counter in the police station, I press the button that is supposed to make someone come out to talk to me, while Bruce is waiting in the car. Then I talk to the lady who appears:

JOHANNES: Hi, could you tell me whether convicted felons are allowed to have any guns?

LADY: Let me check... [*she goes of to call someone and comes back a little later*] No, convicted felons are not allowed to have any firearms whatsoever.

JOHANNES: OK, then I want to file a report on a guy who is a convicted felon who has a gun here in town.

LADY: OK, do you know where he is now?

JOHANNES: Yes, at home. And I have the address...

LADY: OK, could you give it to me?

JOHANNES: yes, it's 1564 E Avenue. And the name is John McConn...

LADY: John McConnell?

[*I am unsure to what degree she repeats the name before I am finished stating it myself.*]

JOHANNES: Yes. John McConnell.

LADY: Oh OK, well I'll tell an officer.

[*The Lady goes off and does not seem to bother about my filing any more.*]

When I get outside, Bruce is still waiting there. I tell him what I did and we decide to go back in because I had forgotten to tell them that John had been discussing the pros and cons of having a shoot-out with the police. Bruce tries to give the whole report some more urgency by talking in a somewhat aggravated voice, and we get the assurance that they will look into the matter.

While we are about to pull out of the parking lot, Bruce's father is pulling up. He is also interested in what is going on, after being disturbed while watching a movie. Bruce and I then drive over to Todd's again. The Barkers think that it is better that I stay away from Todd's house as long as John is still around, because John knows where it is located and he might come after me when he finds out that I reported him. I am invited to stay overnight at the Barkers and then I am going to leave for Joe's place the next morning with Bruce.

I stay with Bruce at Joe's until Wednesday after work. Wednesday morning I start sending e-mails to Art as I know he will be hanging around the library. John is in the library at this time. Sarah calls the police to hear what has happened, but nobody there has heard anything of the police report. They instruct her that if I want to file a police report, I would actually need to talk to an actual police-man and not just the dispatch.

As soon as we are back in Douglas, I go back over to John's place one very last time to offer to take his gun, and to bring it to the police in my backpack without telling them where I found it. When he sees me, he seems astonished. He had asked Kevin where I was, and Kevin had told him I had gone out to some park, while I tell him, that I have been working out at Joe's. I make the offer to turn his gun in and his answer is that his landlord offered him the same thing when he showed the gun to him. At least now I know that I am not the only one who knows about the gun. But John refuses to hand his gun over once more, so I leave for the police station.

The dispatch hears what I am inquiring about, and she tells me to sit down and wait. After waiting for about 45 minutes for a police-man to show up, she informs me that the only two police-men on duty are currently busy, and that I should come back an hour later. I follow her advice and an hour later, I finally get to file a report to a policeman. Or so I think.

As a measure of security, I move to the Barkers, since it is outside of the radius where John goes. Douglas is small though, so there is no way to avoid him while walking around and just a few nights later he sees me walking on the sidewalk in Agua Prieta and decides to hang around me. Then Sarah feels one day that it is time to ask the police why nothing has happened. She calls the police, and one officer comes by the library. In her office, I tell him the story once more, while John is sitting in the children's section of the library where Hoochie, the clown, is giving out candy as a promotion for the upcoming circus night. At this time John has announced that he is going to leave some time in the not too distant future, so Sarah and I think that if a shoot-out is planned, it is probably imminent. The officer does not know how to respond and calls a second officer who is on duty. No police report has been filed as far as they know. "Was he Hispanic?" they want to know about the police-man who took the report. I do not recall.

The next time Sarah contacts the police again, they have stopped by John's house, but since they saw no furniture in his bedroom through the window, they assumed that he had moved on. Sarah points out that some people "just live like that," and the police-man replies by telling her an anecdote about a man who lives in Douglas and is roaming around the streets with nothing but a grocery bag and is living in a nice house where he sleeps on the floor. While Sarah is amused by the story, when she tells it to Bruce, Tom and me, Tom just sneers: "What has that to do with why they haven't arrested John yet?"

After another few days, the police tell us they cannot determine whether or not John is a convicted felon. This is when Edwin Ludszeweit steps in. Edwin talks a lot about his contacts, and he stops on the road in his pickup when I ride by on my bike. "Just stay out in the open," he advises me about meeting John. Edwin calls the police chief and they tell him that they do not have John's police record. The record is public and so Edwin finds it on the Internet himself and provides the police with the Internet address. After finally having the information, the police chief calls Sarah to tell her that 'a concerned citizen' has contacted him and advised him about the seriousness of the case. "You don't happen to have a young foreign student living with you?" the police chief asks. He goes on for a while telling Sarah that she should just call him when John is in the library.

The next day John is at the library again, and Sarah calls the police. But this time unfortunately, all officers on duty are at lunch so none of them can come by. After Edwin contacts them once more, they decide to come down to the library — and undercover they sit and read some newspapers while looking at John. Edwin notices them and drives over to El Espejo to warn me not to go to the library right then. But nothing ever comes out of the case, and John never finds out about any of it.

Analysis

The case of John reveals not only his own attitude toward 'the law' and 'violence' as abstract concepts, but also the view some other layers of Douglas society hold. Summarizing, we can say that John's relation to the law is that it is to be followed if there may be consequences for not following it. On the other hand, his reason for disobeying the law by not turning the gun in to start with, is that the gun might be used against him later on. When he finally decides to follow the law, he silently to be silently acknowledging the power of the state. It is fascinating that he disconnects the concept of obeying the law from the concept of moral responsibility. His constant accusations against the police, saying they are 'crooks,' shows that he acknowledges the direct interest politics that lie in power of the police, although without going as far as taking class-relations in to consideration.

The Barkers, especially Sarah, and Edwin have a high amount of faith in the police system, believing that it will enforce the law. Even though the police do not react to our inquiries, they continue to contact them. It is only after several weeks and many excuses that they realize that the local police have decided not to arrest him. And even after that, Sarah and Edwin discuss the case very little.

The relationship between the police department itself and 'the law' is also quite interesting: If we take it as a given that they are not quite as disorganized and amateurish as they try to portray themselves, their handling of the case did not meet the standard of good law enforcement expected by Edwin and the Barkers. Given that John is not a police agent and that reality is not more complex than what we see on the surface, it is fair to assume that the police do not prioritize pursuing John precisely because he is dangerous, and the enforcement of the law in their eyes is also very dependent on the repercussions they have to fear enforcing it. If that is true, their view of the law is quite similar to John's. Although he might be insane, he understands the police better than anyone else.

Certain aspects of the political-economical view are certainly useful here, for example in giving a background concerning the importance of crime to those employed by the police in relation to their job security. However, the prediction that the law is enforced against the working class seems not to hold true or at least not be applicable to the lumpenproletariat, if one classifies John as such. And although this view gives us an analysis of how crime works in a class society, it does not really help us to explain the situation and why John decides to break the law in the first place.

The structuralist view contributes equally to somewhat explain the situation: There is a certain difference between John's background, which is from a family that is in the lumber business (see — "John", p. 188) and Sarah, who has been working in the public sector both as a teacher and a librarian (see — "Sarah and Tom ", p. 69). However, also this model does not quite explain why John feels so at ease with breaking the law and why he thinks that he is in a situation where the police might start killing him without much concern for the law at all.

Petty Crimes

Some crimes are really too small to be counted as criminal behavior, because one really does not hurt the system by committing them. Often these are things that are done just to make life a little bit easier for the perpetrator. Nevertheless, they do tell us quite a bit about the level of seriousness that is attributed to breaking the law. I will here present two such cases in which the state bureaucracy is circumvented.

The Social Security Scam

During my first week at the Lerman, Mr. Fernandez shows that he is upset that I am running around with my passport all the time and that the border guards therefore do not "recognize me as a U.S. citizen." He thinks I should go and get an Arizona Driver's License and use that instead at the border. Although I object constantly, he insists. I find out that I will need a social security number[1] and as I did receive one while being an exchange student in South Carolina a few years back, I hope I can reuse that number. But unfortunately, I do not know whether the number I remember is the right one. So I go down to the local social security office and ask them to verify my number, and they reply that it is against the law to do that. I go back to the Lerman, thinking that I now have an excuse for not getting the driver's license, so I tell Mr. Fernandez what happened. "Oh, no problem," he gives me a phone number, "call this number and ask there." I dial the number and a southern black female voice answers. I ask her the same question that the local lady said she was not allowed to answer and I add a few "ma'am"s whenever it seems possible to do so, and yes, she does confirm my social security number. I also get the South Carolina Department of Motor Vehicles (DMV)[2] to send my driving record and get a driver's license at the local MVD[3]. "See, I told you," Mr. Fernandez tells me. I continue using my passport for crossing the border, although Mr. Fernandez thinks that is silly: "Just say you are U.S.!"

Registering Cars

Another instance of something that is officially considered a crime is the way Art has to use his car. He tells me the story the first time we meet at the library. He wanted to sell a book and so he drove from California to North Carolina. In North Carolina his car was

---

[1] The soc.sec. is a number that almost all U.S. citizens have which must be used for employment and taxation, but also for voter registration and other services which require a national numbering system.

[2] The DMV is an office that can be found in most towns and is run by the individual state. It is responsible for giving out licenses and registering vehicles.

[3] The Motor Vehicle Division is Arizona's version of a DMV.

hit by another car, and so they paid him money so he could buy a new car, although it would be less expensive than the last one. He bought the car at a used car dealer that was "pretty crappy," as he says. He then wondered whether he needed to register the car in North Carolina, but at the local DMV they tell him that he can use the California plates from his old car. "That is legal at least to the border of North Carolina," is what they said, according to Art.

When Art then drove back to California, he was stopped by the highway patrol; in California it is not legal to reuse old plates. Art had lost the car papers in the meantime and he was quite sure that the car dealer in North Carolina would not remember him either. So he has been driving around without plates ever since. "It goes fine if you just drive at night and when you get stopped you show them some paper that you are in the process of applying," Art says in January, when he is still living in it. At night he drives around Douglas and parks at certain places at certain times where he assumes they will not catch him. At 5am he drives to the last location, and then he can drive back to the parking lot behind the library at 10am. After some time, they manage to catch him anyway, and he is ordered to go to court unless he manages to get a license before the court date. For a license, he needs an insurance policy for which he does not have money, and he needs to prove that he owns the car with the papers he no longer has.

After his court date, they grant him a temporary license for about three months, so the last months he is living at the Lerman, Art no longer drives his car at all. He could have received a real license if he had filed the car as being abandoned, because they would then give him a paper of ownership after a few days and then he could receive an insurance policy. But Art thinks that it is not worth bothering with. Instead he uses his car as storage space and as long as he can park it behind the Lerman, the police do not bother him.

Analysis

As this passage shows us, both Art and Mr. Fernandez have a very 'relaxed' attitude to the law: if one can get services one should take them no matter whether one is entitled to them or not, and one is obliged to follow the law only so far as one is actually threatened with a penalty. This view seems similar to John's, in which we just saw a total lack of moral obligation to follow the law. At the same time, the cases in which they encounter conflict with the law are not as violent and any penalties would take place through the state bureaucracy and not direct armed confrontation with law enforcement officers.

Also in these examples, the class-relations aspect is not quite discernible in the enforcement of the law, and certainly it is hard to see how it is forcing "workers into submission." The political-economical view therefore adds little to the understanding of the driving forces that make the two willing to break the law. An analysis of the long-term class background of the two would probably also reveal that they have learned which laws can be circumvented and which ones can not, but there seems to be little connection between the rules that the two may have carried over from some work place — as neither of them talk about having a history of working in a factory.

Again, we see that the two Marxist models are not able to explain very much in this situation.

Street kids

One night I walk around the 8th Street Park and there are a few kids drinking something I cannot discern. I walk by, but quickly realize that it probably was alcohol, which is outlawed in this particular park. Now that I have an excuse to start talking to them, I turn around and head back to them. "Didn't you have some alcohol here a few minutes ago?" I ask, not thinking about the fact that these are probably minors who are not allowed to drink alcohol at all. They deny my claim and quickly disperse, and I walk on. A few minutes later, three boys come running towards me from three directions, surrounding me, as I am about to leave the Park. "I heard you asked them for liquor and you said you wanted to touch my girlfriends' tit!" one of them starts, "I am David Dell— I practically own this town." They expect me to be an undercover agent. David makes it clear that I do not want to "mess with [him]," as practically anything can happen to me, since he has control over the politic system and all the cops in town. David believes in my explanation about not having asked about touching his girlfriend's tit, but he still wants prove that I am not an undercover cop. I tell them my story, and offer to show my German passport if they will not take it away from me. They immediately understand my dilemma, and all three of them put their hands in their armpits, which prevents them from taking my passport while I show it to them. They do it without communicating with one another, so they must do this quite often, I conclude. After I have shown it to them, they lighten up. "Listen, I have a party tomorrow night," David explains, "if you wanna come, you are invited. Just don't do this 'I am English' [gesticulating how he believes an upper class British person moves his hand] shit!" I ask for directions, and they are all very eager to explain them. David makes sure to mention that there will be lots of girls for me to "check out."

Not wanting to go to a teenagers' party all alone, I convince Bruce to come with me and he tries to look younger by putting on his hood. The party is in the back yard with about 100 teenagers all drinking beer. David introduces me to different people as "a guy from Russia who writes a book on Douglas," and several of them want Bruce and me to rap something in Russian or some other language. "I always expected them to ask me to say something in Louisianan," Bruce says afterwards, as they seem not to have realized that Louisiana, the state that Bruce went to college in, is part of the United States. David starts sending girls over to us, and the first candidate is Wanda, as she "is white," David explains. Unfortunately, Wanda is completely off into a dream state as the result of the use of some drug. After a while, the headlights of a car can be seen behind the fence of the garden. Teenagers start running inside the house, and several of them start jumping over fences towards the front and the neighboring house. Bruce is standing still with his beer, but I fear that we might probably be charged with something given that all the others are minors, so we slowly walk off towards his parents' house.

When I meet David a few days later, he asks: "What happened? Why did you go so early?" I explain that we thought the police was about to bust his party, but he tells me: "No, no, I just went back there and told them I had a party going on and they went away. I told you I have control with them cops, didn't I?" He then goes on to explain that he controls several cars that drive around Douglas and that if I want to go anywhere, I should just yell when one of them drives by so they can pick me up.

Analysis

I believe this example shows that the relaxed view of the law I recorded among several of my main informants is not just limited to a small minority with unusual viewpoints, but also mirrors ideas held by wider parts of the population. The view that the police are very corrupt is also strongly held by David and his friends. Differing from the group of Anglos who I mostly study, they claim to have also built up elaborate power structures to bypass the law, including the local police force in the scheme. To what degree these structures actually exist, and to what degree they exist only in the imagination of the teenagers is hard to determine from the behavior of the police. The fact that they break the law by drinking in the U.S. when they might have easily partied in Mexico to avoid legal problems shows their alternative structures have at least some power, although they might not be quite as strong as David would like.

Now this may recall Douglas' former status as a company town, which has left traces of that culture in the way parents educate their children and how those children behave. Structural factors only explain slightly more in this situation than in those previously mentioned. Except for Bruce, who is different in many other ways including class background, there is no clear class division among the kids in the question of whether they will or will not follow the law. The political-economical view explains even less; unless one believes David that the party was not broken up because of his influence as part of a powerful family in Douglas.

Registering Foreign Voters

When I am about to move in at Todd's place, and I meet him for the handover of the key, the Arizona primaries are about to come up. Todd's introductory question is: "So have you registered to vote already?" I thought he knew I was a foreigner, but I tell him once again, just to make sure as I cannot otherwise explain why he would have asked such a question. "So what?" is his answer, "vote early, vote often!" And with a broad smile, Todd tells me that I should just go and register to vote; there cannot be any harm in that. "Basically, I am not supposed to vote at all 'cause of my probation, but at one time I was registered in two counties, and I voted absentee in the other one," he goes on. I continue listening to him for a while but I do not take him very seriously, as I am sure there must be mechanisms in place to prevent foreigners from voting. It will take some months for me to realize that I am quite wrong.

Todd does not stop there. He also tells me to apply for a passport when I move in at his place. "But you need a U.S. birth certificate," he says. He himself used to be called Gordon Daniels, but he did not like the sound of his first name, so instead of applying for name change through the usual channels, he forged a birth certificate for himself that stated he was born in Jersey City, New Jersey with a new name. During my time there, he starts considering making another birth certificate in the name of "Todd Nieldas" as it would sound a bit more exotic. Unfortunately, the equipment to make these fake birth certificates is stored somewhere further South in Mexico, so he cannot get to it right away.

After Todd has told me this, the whole matter is quickly forgotten for a few months, until the incident with Jesper comes up. Jesper is a Danish exchange student at Cochise College, and he also stayed at the Lerman to begin with, but moved to the Grand after a few weeks. I do not see him much, but one evening he talks to Todd, Art and me on Todd's porch about going to Agua Prieta to see the nightlife.

Art tells us what happened at the Lerman that day: Mr. Fernandez came into the Lerman lobby with a big smile — he had just received Jesper's registration card for the U.S. Selective Service[4]. Since Jesper is not living there anymore, Mr. Fernandez handed the card to Art. "It's going to be real interesting to see how he's

---

[4]The draft system in the United States is at this time is only registering young males through the Selective Service system, but is not actually drafting anyone.

going get out of that one," Art tells Todd and they both smile at us. First, Jesper seems seriously disturbed. His application for a driver license has somehow triggered the U.S. military to think that he is a U.S. citizen. The next day he goes down to the migration office at the border so they can take a look at his passport and verify that he is a foreigner who is not supposed to get drafted. According to them, he shows them his passport and his accompanying visa. But the answer he gets from the migration officer just stuns him: "Well, just because you have a foreign passport and a visa... that is no proof that you are not a U.S. citizen."

Art and Todd now both urge him on to go and register to vote. He adds: "Now I'm going for Food Stamps!" Art agrees, but he does not seem to really mean it. A few days later Jesper actually registers to vote with his social security number just to see if there is not a whistle going off now, which will at least produce a document stating that he is not a U.S. citizen. Several months later, a few days before he is to leave the U.S., his voter registration card arrives in the mail at the Lerman Hotel. Mr. Fernandez hands it to Art without much astonishment, and Art just casually tells me one day at the library while creating some electric circuit from spare parts: "Oh, by the way, Jesper's voter registration came in yesterday." Art is hanging around Stan a lot at the time, and so Stan, preoccupied with other thoughts, also quickly gives his comment on the matter: "Oh."

I call Bruce and tell him Jesper's voter registration has come in, which he does not understand, because he cannot believe it before he actually sees the card. "You know you could go to prison," he tells Jesper when he sees him at the library the next time. Meanwhile Todd is celebrating the event, since it shows the ineffectiveness and chaotic character of the government. It only takes a few days for Bruce to start suggesting that Jesper should also apply for a passport that he would ship to him "if the application goes through and it ever arrives."

Art's secondary reaction is quite different: "That is democracy in action! ... We need to get all of AP to register to vote like that! ... That is how elections can be won: millions of young Europeans on holiday over here register to vote." When Jesper shows the voter registration to Jeff at the library, I am sitting at the table next to them. Jesper tells him about the background of it, and Jeff asks: "Did you get your driver license here in Douglas? ... Yeah they always screw things up like that." When Jesper shows it to Edwin a few minutes later, Edwin says in a low voice: "Now you don't want to show that to everyone, you don't know what those Nazis in charge are up to." Although Jesper totally stops telling anyone about it, the news spreads quickly, and by the time my good-bye party is held, everyone knows about it.

Edwin's wife responds: "Well there aren't many who go vote anyways," implying that as Americans do not vote, it is not so problematic to let foreigners vote. Todd just says: "The most frequent voters in Douglas live in the graveyard — they use mail-in ballots."

The whole matter triggers Todd's idea of forging birth certificates again, and while it is being discussed at El Espejo, Kevin questions the usefulness of it: "Is it really worth it?" Todd agrees that it really is not worth it for a European to get an American citizenship to gain materially, and that it is more just a matter of tricking the system. "They'll never be able to synchronize those databases," he predicts.

Analysis

Although all people I talk to approve of the fact that Jesper can vote at the elections, the main difference in the reactions is between those like Art and Todd who have lost all faith in the law and only see this as a part of an individual's strategy to obtain certain rights, and those like the Barkers and Edwin and his wife who still hold a distinction between lawful and unlawful actions. However, both groups subscribe to the idea that one should only avoid doing something if one has a chance of being caught.

This belief can hardly be due to Art's and Todd's long-term employment as blue-collar workers, as the structuralist view would predict, because they both have largely avoided that kind of work over the years. It was rather in the process of spurning those kinds of jobs that they have acquired their subversive characteristics. The political-economical view also looks rather irrelevant, since employment, once again, is not an issue in this town.

Copying Music

In addition to the crimes that are specific to Douglas, there are also certain youth crimes that have become ubiquitous. One day, when Bruce's brother Robert is visiting his family, Bruce, Robert, and I sit in Bruce's room downloading music and videos from the Internet on our laptops. "Now is that legal?" Sarah inquires when she pops her head in. No answer. "I've heard that they drive around catching people that copy music illegally," Sarah continues. "Ah, no one actually believes that shit," is Bruce's response, and none of us make any further comments about it, but Sarah keeps standing in the doorway unsure how to proceed. Later on that day I am able to hear Sarah's complete opinion on the matter. She believes it is stealing "if one takes something that one does not own." I try to argue that it is the current mode of production that limits the amount of music that can be listened to. It artificially limits the number of available songs, because only those who pay for them may listen to them while the process of digital copying could easily make it available for everyone. For that, the state would have to fund a lot of scholarships for all those who want to produce music so that they are not dependent on profits made from their music. Sarah follows my reasoning, but she thinks that to be fair, to the government should set up such scholarships before people are allowed to copy for free.

   None of the younger people I talk to see a problem with copying music though, and one of the Cyber Teens asks me to burn two CDs for him of his favorite songs, because he does not have the Internet at home. However, the college student Carmelo tells me: "See I would download music, but I have a friend who got caught." And generally the youngsters still buy some CDs on their trips to nearby cities.

Analysis

This example shows the ineffectiveness of trying to separate class differences between those who obey the law and those who do not. Instead, it is age that comes into play here, as all the younger kids have less belief in the moral requirement to follow the law and the government's ability to enforce the law across all class boundaries. Of course, very affluent teens should have the ability to buy all their CDs legally, but none of my informants really fall into this category. Structural factors explain very little here. On the other hand, copying music might be forbidden in the first place due to the political-economical surroundings — as it is in the interest of the ruling class to do so. However, with few or if any ruling class individuals visible in Douglas, this does not really tell us why the law is not being taken more seriously by the younger generation.

Final Analysis — how helpful were the two existing approaches?

The structure of society may cause a lot of the behavior of the youngsters, many of which have parents or grandparents who used to work at the smelter or the mine. Their positions were to a large degree competitive, and although white-collar bureaucratic positions did exist, these were reserved for the Anglo middle class, which had moved away together with the jobs. Also Kevin has a similar idea when he says that Douglas has a company town mentality in which people are afraid of repression if they dare stand up publicly against the mayor.

However, this is not a complete explanation. Neither John nor Art have ever had any connection to Phelps Dodge, and the Barkers also arrived later on. The explanation has to be found at a deeper level of current consciousness that cannot be determined only by analyzing the production relations of one generation ago.

Trying to use the political-economical view to explain the cases observed in Douglas, we immediately find some applicability. The law is certainly enforced selectively and crime is certainly only defined as crime if the local law enforcement officers decide to do so, and also just about any behavior has the potential to be defined as criminal. Further, by providing jobs to the lumpenproletariat, which comprises such a great part of Douglas' population, crime also has its effect, probably best exemplified by a quote Kevin has from an unknown source:

> In Douglas you either earn your money in law enforce-
> ment or by breaking the law — or both.

And also, according to the stories mainly older Anglos tell me, when Douglas was industrialized, the law was enforced much more thoroughly.

It is harder to prove the extent to which the law is enforced against the working class and not the ruling class. The ruling class of one of the major employers, Wal-Mart, is not living in Douglas at all, and it is uncertain to what degree the mayor has influence over Food City. And also, it is questionable whether crime takes away people's attention from class exploitation. Just about all who are in a working class position are involved in some form of crime themselves. It is only people like Sarah, working in the ideological class, who appear to see morality connected to the law in at least some areas.

And while certainly helpful, the political-economical perspective cannot tell us much about the reasons that might lead people to break the law; the question of state legitimacy is not taken into consideration.

Conclusion — The State Legitimacy Perspective

As we can see, the two traditional Marxist models we have looked at fall short at explaining and analyzing the criminal behavior that is conducted in Douglas. But this should not lead us to abandon the Marxist framework altogether as a helpful tool to analyze the situation — it just has to be done with a new approach that is appropriate for fragmented and transient societies that are missing the ruling capitalist class and where a large percentage of the population is from other areas and therefore missing local family traditions

In order to understand why Mr. Fernandez is willing to step across the line to the illegal in order to get me food stamps or why Todd and Art and others do not see any moral problem with Jesper requesting a voter registration, we must examine the issue of state legitimacy. It is the state itself with all its laws, that is illegitimate in their view. Although not all of them agree on the

Photo: Johannes Wilm

Picture 13: The Douglas border entrance. Fire arms are 'forbidden' in Mexico.

same political ideology, they agree on the idea that crimes, at least "harmless" ones, are permissible. John shows his resentment toward the authorities, when we walk to Food City one day:

> You know, every once in a while, this country is run by crooks. Then we need to straighten things up...a few people will have to be jailed, a few people will have to be executed. But it will be done. Then the crooks are gone for a while and they slowly move back in. [...] Right now we are at such a point where everything is run by crooks, like the water supply and city management everywhere and the federal government [...] and all those Americans that are in jail at the Marine bases and all those foreigners that are taking over the military. [...] The Army needs to go from town to town and straighten things up.

While John believes that most of law enforcement personnel are immoral, he does not see any way of removing them from power other than to use military force to remove them, blatantly sidestepping the law. This is combined with a heavy dose of nationalism, and although the exact wording is very particular to John, I believe the statement mirrors some of the main lines of thought among many of my informants.

The fact that the Barker parents are not involved in any of the practice defined as illegal can give an indication that there is a certain class basis for this view: only from a certain level can one afford not to have an ideology that permits crimes to a certain extend. But this relationship is not deterministic; also Bruce offered to apply for a passport on Jesper' behalf, and some of the kids I talk to who come from poorer households hold strong ideologies that are inexcusable of crimes — January is an example thereof.

In *The German Ideology*, Marx talks more directly about crime than he does in *The Capital*. According to Marx, criminal events are only purely arbitrary in the view of idealists. Laws, for Marx, are determined not just by the will of the people, but by a combination of will and what is materially possible at the given stage of development. The general will of the people usually fits the development stage in matters of what is feasible at the time, and only idealists think independently of the current development stage. Therefore, they see the general will of the people at any given time as completely arbitrary. If people no longer respect the law of the state, this is a reflection not only of the will of the people having changed, but also of a change in the quality of life of the individual. The people might not even have experienced this change, but simply inherited the law from generations before them. Such laws are no longer ruling laws, but rather nominal laws. (Engels and Marx 1974, 106–107)

Different from Marx's description, the laws that are nominal for some members of society are still ruling laws for other parts. And in Douglas, the level of crime has historically always been high, given its geographic location, but since Phelps Dodge closed the crime level has increased.

One could argue that in Douglas, a segment of the population has evolved that has material conditions different from most of the rest of the country, due to the lack of local production and its geographic location on the border. Because of these material conditions, many of the laws are no longer the general wish of the people and they turn into nominal laws. But as the country is not homogeneous, this is only the case for a small sector of the nation. On the other hand, consider the illegal music sharing: might Douglas simply be leading the way for the rest of the country?

One factor in community building is the common disagreement with the given laws that are otherwise accepted by society at large. The result is that children growing up in Douglas are socialized into this way of thinking, and Douglas attracts people from other parts of the country who have a similar view.

Partially, this falls in line with observations that the high amount of criminal activity in borderlands has a tendency to subvert and undermine the state's institutions (Donnan and Wilson 1999, 88).

However, it is often held that the activities rarely have revolutionary goals, as the smuggling business depends on the fact that it is illegal (Donnan and Wilson 1999, 88). Now this is a link that I either have not seen or does not exist in Douglas; those involved in criminal activity are not very much concerned about the fact that their activity might hurt, or ultimately destroy, the state they live in. This has to be weighed against the historical fact that there had been quite a lot of revolutionary activity in the area. Agua Prieta had hosted several armed struggles in the years 1911 to 1929, and U.S. federal troops were stationed in Douglas in order to contain the revolutionary energy in Mexico (Jeffrey 1951, 52). Jeffrey (1951, 55–61) shows by the example of the rebel leader 'Red' López, that it was the close proximity to the border that gave the revolutionaries the opportunity to trick the Mexican federal troops by crossing the border.

Likewise, labor organizing by the outspoken revolutionary union *Industrial Workers of the World* (IWW) was particularly strong in Bisbee in 1917, with demands of ending discriminatory pay and employment practices against members of ethnic minorities, because the union was better than its reformist counterparts in organizing Hispanic workers together with Anglo workers. Over half of Bisbee's work force broke out in strike when the employers did not comply with the union's demand, and the whole situation was not defused before "vigilante-groups" deported 1186 striking miners to New Mexico. (Bonnand 1997)

People in borderlands often are "doubly peripheralized" as they will be both on the margins of the economy and of the state (Donnan and Wilson 1999, 88). Now why would these people, living under the worst conditions in their country, actively make sure that their actions do not subvert the state power entirely more so than any other subversive force? And since each individual can only subvert a tiny amount on his own, and even a large family network on its own has no chance of subverting the state, how can they ever know that their particular action created the turning point that completely subverted the state institutions?

However, on the empirical grounds there are generally few revolutions are planned compared to the amount of ordinary crime that is happening in most borderlands, just as in most interior areas, there are very few revolutionaries most of the time.

Again Marx can help us with a model, this time from his general analysis of capitalism and capitalists: although it is in the interest of the entire capitalist class to keep the working class up to a standard of living that will enable them to reproduce to maintain the labor force and to buy enough goods to avoid having an excess of production, it is in the interest of the single capitalist to minimize labor costs and maximize the price of his products. If we assume that it is in the interest of the people living near the border to maintain the state power, a similar model here could be that it is in the interest of all the smugglers as a group to have a semi-effective border control in place, but it is in the interest of each individual who is breaking the law that he specifically is never caught and prosecuted.

Chapter 5

War & Nationalism

NATIONALISM mainly builds on the idea of nations being some kind of community. Most critics hold that these are only 'imagined communities.' They are imagined in the sense that no one actually ever sees all other members and therefore cannot know whether all of them actually have anything/something in common at all (Anderson 1991).

While, most critics' transcendence of the nation category consists mainly of looking at how knowledge varies amongst individuals within a nation, Marxists emphasize the differing objective material interests of the various classes and fractions of classes within a nation. Each fraction has in fact more material interests in common with similar classes and fractions in other nations — and nationalism hides all this.

In Douglas, this difference of interests seems obvious, not between different factions of the city's population, but between most Douglasites and a few people in other parts of the country. Douglasites enlist in the Armed Services and fight in wars more often than the average, and it is not in most Douglasites particular interest to be in those wars. But because employment within law enforcement is one of the few occupations that are available other than criminal activity, military recruiters are a common sight in Douglas.

The recruiter

The number of Douglasites who go to war for "their country" is 14 times the national average according to Bruce, who has done some research on the matter. Going to war for your country is probably by most seen as a duty that comes with being a member of a nation that has decided to go to war. In contrast to the rights that one can extract from membership in a nation, or 'citizenship' as it is often called, fulfilling such duties has to be based on either ideological or material grounds. Typically that involves a nationalistic ideology and sometimes includes religion, while materialistic grounds are usually an urgently needed paycheck and future benefits such as college tuition subsidies.

Sgt. Skinner is one of the recruiters. He comes to the library up to several times a week. Most days he is wearing his uniform, and I usually try to sit as close to him as possible. At first sight, his only tactic is to build up an aura of "coolness" around himself — he listens to loud heavy metal music, he drives his car with the windows rolled down while wearing large black sun glasses, and when he talks to the youngsters, he makes sure to show off his cell phone and his laptop. Once, I notice how he throws the cell phone over his shoulder to a candidate, who needs to call his mother to ask for permission to join, while he is walking across the street to a copy shop. Sgt. Skinner looks like he might be in his thirties, but that might largely be part of his "young" image and he is completely bald — he really might be well into his fifties. From Jeff I learn that Sgt. Skinner is a member of the Republican Party, but that he does not "really believe in the ideals of conservatism;" instead it is just to gain in power inside the military. On his laptop, Sgt. Skinner has some kind of test to determine whether the candidate's English skills are adequate. The program might also test other skills, but I only witness the result of a language test. It is a boy and a girl from AP; I believe they are brother and sister. She just parsed through the English exam without any problem when I enter, but he does not make it. Sgt. Skinner advises:

> OK, well that does not mean that you cannot join. But what you will have to do is to go to an English course in Tucson first. [...] You are going to have your own room

with a bed and a TV and a phone and there are going to
be three meals a day. [...] But there is one problem with
the course: The majority of those there are going to be
female. So there is going a lot partying going on... You
just have to make sure not to party too much. You need
to attend classes as well.

Both by this statement and by constantly showing off his laptop
and mobile phone, he is not only trying to show that he is cool,
but also that the ARMY will give the candidates access to a level
of wealth that they otherwise would not be able to ever attain.
In addition, he is exploiting their sex drive to get young boys to
join. As Kevin says: "People here are only going to Disneyland for
holidays, or Las Vegas. They never get out, except if they join the
ARMY."

Kevin's statement is quite interesting: while he himself undeni-
ably is a U.S. citizen, and one might expect that he would follow a
U.S. nationalist ideology, the opposite is the case.

And it is also not just mere coincidence. One day, after a home
coming parade for Douglas soldiers that have served in Iraq, I
finally get to talk to an actual soldier who has served in Iraq. It is a
Hispanic father, who comes by El Espejo with his entire family. He
has only arrived back in Douglas recently, and obviously seems still
disturbed by his experience. Unfortunately therefore, he does not
want to talk about it very much. "Seen too many dead children,"
he explains, while he almost starts to cry. However, he finds time
to comment on the low number of Anglos in the military. "I guess
white people don't like serving their country that much," as he
puts it.

Douglas graduates

Graduation time is the time when Douglasites have to decide upon
what to do in life — and the military is one of the most common
options.

Maria considers joining the ARMY but she does not actually
sign up, as "it's way too dangerous these days," at least during my
two visits to Douglas. Only nine months after my second trip does

Photo: Johannes Wilm

Picture 14: This is a happy day. Douglas soldiers have returned from Iraq.

Photo: Johannes Wilm

Picture 15: Children in a parade celebrating Douglas soldiers

she make an appointment with Sgt. Skinner, after her friend Lynn has died of an overdose, and she explains that she is "so desperate to get out of here [...] even if I have to go to war."

Not so with January, who comes to the library up to a few times a week. She has already signed up a few months before I arrive during senior year and Sgt. Skinner allegedly came to her birthday party. Both her parents are from Mexico, and they work on the Mexican side of the border as doctors and live on the American side. January's older sister is studying and has a child with her boyfriend. All three of them live at January's parents' house, and January explains that she does not want to burden her family in the same way. But in addition to this material reasoning, January also explains that she supports a draft, even if it goes against some of the civil liberties declared in the Bill of Rights[1]. She explains her view by pointing to an extreme alternative — the country itself might disappear, and then "all the rights are gone." January also sees a problem in the way things are currently run, because rich people are taxed too much, religion is being banned more and more from public institutions, and in a few years 25% of the U.S. population will be Hispanic, which in her opinion makes national unity difficult. Regarding foreign policy, she comments: "You know, I don't think the U.S. should be going everywhere, but I like the 'big stick' policy." At one point she briefly has doubts about her engagement in the ARMY one day when she says: "You know, one thing is to die for your country, but another thing is to kill for your country. Would you be able to do that?" she asks her friend Lisa, who sits besides her.

Lisa has a Mexican mother and a father from the U.S. . She sees herself as 'liberal', while January sees herself a conservative. Lisa also sees January as being conservative. Lisa does not want to join the military, but her cousin is planning on joining. Lisa's parents are very much against the Iraq War and they are neighbors of the Barkers. Bruce and I get invited there once by walking up to the front door while her father pulls up from behind.

Some weeks later, Lisa is explaining her view of life in an e-mail:

---

[1] The *Bill of Rights* contains the first ten Amendments to the U.S. Constitution. These amendments define most of the basic personal rights such as freedom of speech.

The way you got to look at life is like this, it's solely up to you. Everything in the world is up to you. If you wish to be competitive then you'll find people to compete against, if you wish to be really nice then you'll always find people to help, if you wish to be mean then you'll always find people to step on. Maybe it could best be summed up by saying "if you think therefore you are". You are your own world. If you are the best looking person in your own world then therefore you are. Nobody else's world matters.[2]

Another few weeks later she writes another criticism. This time she comes to the conclusion that I must clearly be a 'hater' of America:

Usually when someone is constantly making negative remarks that generalize you into a certain group of people then for some reason you become proud. You become proud to be the underdog. And I am a very liberal person, meaning that I always question the actions of the United States, but I have become proud. I have realized that it's people like you who are the glue to Americans, through haters we learn to live together and be proud.

Bruce's reaction to the mail when he hears about it is: "What a bunch of crap. That is just the same old Fox News kind of stuff." But he does not think Lisa is very nationalistic in general, "she probably just isn't used to hear it coming from foreigners." When I tell Edwin about it, he responds: "That is just one of the Douglas fascists." Todd and Kevin think it is funny, especially when I try to rectify my "Anti-Americanism" by trying to focus on positive aspects. The day I am to leave, the Barkers give me a t-shirt saying "I love USA," and they also offer me a t-shirt saying "United We Stand," that Sarah got from the city as a city employee, but that she refuses to ever wear.

---

[2]The excerpt is part of a longer heated debate about competition in the U.S., but I think it makes sense to read by itself.

Another aspect is that I had not considered Douglas to be strongly a part of the U.S. The Barkers, who I saw as Americans, also do not see most of Douglas as staunchly American, but as incorporating foreign cultural traits. It is also interesting that when Lisa feels she is glued together with other Americans, this certainly does not include many of the self-marginalized Anglos who are living in Douglas to try to escape some of the assimilation of all Americans into a system of slavery controlled by big corporations, as they see it.

But she is not alone with the view that Douglas is completely part of the United States. Jeff, January's boyfriend, sends me an e-mail criticizing me for having come to Douglas without really getting to know the U.S.. I had never thought I would get to know the U.S. more than I knew it before by living in Douglas. Because of its geographic location alone it cannot be very descriptive of the average American small town.

Jeff describes himself as conservative and is avoided by the members of the Maria group, a group of youngsters who listen to a certain genre of music that, among other things, advocates avoiding the law (see also — "Bruce goes to Tucson", p. 101) and that does not put much emphasis on "doing well," the way mainstream society defines it.

One of the more extreme aspects of Jeff's conservatism surfaces when the subject turns to slavery, and Lincoln's famous quote that he would free as many or as few slaves necessary to save the union comes up, Jeff defends him:

> See, Lincoln was morally against slavery. But he also wasn't just going to become president and say, because of my ideals I'm changing everything. This was of course a time when slavery was accepted by a lot of the country. So those words you sent me [in a previous e-mail] have nothing to do with his moral stance. They have to do with what he thought was best for the country, period.

What is important for "the country" is very important for Jeff. According to him, there was no election fraud in 2000 and it was right to attack Afghanistan after 9/11. Arnold Schwarzenegger's speech at the Republican National Convention (RNC) 2004 about how he as a person from socialist Austria could escape to the United States and do it big as a proof that any immigrant from Guatemala can do it as well (Schwarzenegger 2004), was a really good speech. "This is a guy with 'street credit'," Jeff says. Also, according to Jeff, the big problem with having a universal health care system is that it would take away money from "good defense." I cannot help thinking that meanwhile, 'illegal' immigrants are dying almost daily within a few miles in their attempts to enter the United States.

The Maria group sees the other group as being conformist, although they also differentiate among each other. Jeff once describes most other teenagers in Douglas who are not conservative as "hating their parents."

Jeff is the only one from his group who I talk about the Maria group with. He sees them as being losers who are just lazy and who have only themselves to blame for "where they have come in their life." Jeff himself says about his own career plans: "I would like to be a screenwriter/director." He then specifies that it is not just a wish, but for him a realistic goal: "And I'm not someone who is just saying that, that is what I want my sole occupation to be someday."

To the best of my knowledge Jeff, Oscar, Lisa and Carolina have more money available than many others their age. Jeff, Lisa and Carolina come from comparatively wealthy backgrounds, while Oscar has received an unknown sum of money as a result of his injury. Still, Jeff and Oscar completely deny the financial ground they stand on, while those in the Maria group accept their "fate" to a much higher degree and therefore have a realistic outlook of where they can go in life, given the current system and their material constraints. Although those in the Maria group have a higher level of class-consciousness, this does not lead to open rebellion against the structures of society. "The Army and police are too strong," Maria explains. Their rebellion in the form of music is therefore an experiment of following a counter-culture, and they are able to reject the prevalence of a culture that is celebrating the country in a nationalistic way.

One can wonder whether members of the Jeff group simply do not perceive their own status in U.S. society, or whether they do realize it and just tune it out in self-denial. Fact is however, that January never actually joins the military. She tells the recruiter a few days before she is to leave that she has reconsidered her options. And on my second trip to Douglas, she explains her final decision as just a result of a mood that she had at the moment, rather than any change in her opinion on the role of the military.

War is Over

Besides the youngsters, who see joining the military as an option that might lie in their immediate future, there are those who have experienced war by fighting in it. Bicycle Peter, Edwin, Bob Waczkovic and Garry Mora have all been in either Korea or Vietnam. And Todd has been in the Vietnam War as reporter for the L.A. Times. And then those who have not, such as Bruce or Kevin's traveling friend Cosmic Peter, nevertheless have similar outlooks.

The Anti-Nationals

Those I call 'anti-nationals' here do not all agree completely and they have come to their conclusions in different ways. Nevertheless, there is enough commonality among them to group these people together.

   On of the more theoretical anti-nationals is Cosmic Peter. When the newspaper is read at El Espejo one morning, Cosmic Peter (see also p. 195) shows his fatalistic views. "Why don't they just bomb the whole thing?" he asks. Peter does not really think that the U.S. should bomb Iraq all to pieces, but he wants to show that there is just about no chance to change society. He tells about the fact that there are actually pro-war demonstrations in the U.S. and that "at least in Germany people demonstrate against stuff like that." The entire U.S. Presidential election process disgusts Peter:

> So wait a minute, this guy is waging a war. And this other guy is supposed to be the opponent. And he is also for the war.
>
> [...]

Oh, I get it, we can choose between either waging war
with this guy or waging war with this guy. Now that is
a choice!

[…]

The left is always just accepting reality as it is presented
by the right-wingers: first they want to start a war and
it is all clear that Saddam doesn't have the weapons
right then. Then the war starts and no weapons are
found and now suddenly the left argues: "Well the war
was started on just ground because we thought he had
weapons, but now we see that it is not working and that
it was a mistake we all made together."

No it was not! There were no weapons ever and everyone knew that!

I agree with him that the left is accepting the constant redefi-
nition of historical facts by the right, while Kevin and Todd think
over the matter and to interpret the consequences if it were true.
I suggest that the background for this strategy is that the liberals
want to convert those who were wrong while giving them an alibi
for previously having held a wrong opinion. Further, the strategy
will not work, as one should instead point to the consistency in
one's own argument to convince people. Peter agrees.

Much along the lines of the Maria group, it is Peter's belief that
all one can do these days is to "free oneself" from the norms that
society attempts to impose; resistance to the system at large is not
possible given the overwhelming power of the state and the media.

Another viewpoint is presented by Edwin, who originally called
himself conservative. Edwin talks quite a bit about his experiences
in Germany and Korea, and he says he does not know anyone
who had to kill someone in a war that did not "lose his senses"
afterwards. He, as well as the rest of the cultural elite, is very much
against the war in Iraq and once I give him my e-mail address, I start
receiving various news articles on where the Bush administration
"screwed something up" in relation with the war. He sends his
e-mail out to a list of people, and the members of this list vary
depending on the exact topic. On some European issues, it is only

his son in Munich and me who are listed as recipients. On other issues, it is a list of some 30–40 people who receive his e-mails.

Bicycle Peter provides another perspective. He did not mind the attack on him during the Korean War as much as the military's mistreatment of him as a person with feelings. After being transferred to Japan (see — "Bicycle Peter", p. 206), Peter engaged in relationships with two different prostitutes. One of them, Xiau Phan was a "professional prostitute and a wonderful woman." They "lived together happily for a number of years," and during that time, "she quit doing all that," as he tells me.

He wanted to marry her, but "when they [the military] found out I was serious, they shipped me right off. It didn't take them a week!" Peter explains somewhat annoyed. Peter sees it as "a love story and a tragedy, as so many of our lives were back then."

Peter tried to get back, but they would not let him and he didn't have the means to go back to Japan himself.

And then there is the case of John. John never went to the military, but he has quite some experience with guns from other places (see also — "John's got a gun", p. 123). He explains what is going to happen in case of war, addressing Jesper, a European who just received a Selective Service Card due to a computer error (see also p. 135):

> See, when war breaks out, I am assigned to the post office. All the mail needs to be delivered in wartime as well, you know, and I can't really go out fighting anyways. [...] But I'll count on you defending us!

When Jesper suggests that he should ask Sgt. Skinner whether his Selective Service Card has any relevance, John tells him that is probably a bad idea. "They probably placed him at the library just to get you," John suggests, "they will probably take you in any day now [...] If you feel that strongly about not going, you probably should go back to Denmark again." When Jesper goes to ask Sgt. Skinner anyways, John is sitting at the library by pure coincidence and he decides to comment on Sgt. Skinner's "swim belt" for about half an hour while sitting a single meter away from him. A few days later, Art and I talk about the need for national defense. John comments:

> You know, I wouldn't mind if a foreign country was to invade the U.S. . As long as none of my family or anybody I know gets hurt.

> Them Koreans moving in with them little Honda choppers over San Diego [...] I wouldn't mind, as long as nobody I know gets hurt.

Still later, when I ask John whether he ever wants to go back to Arkansas, he answers that he wants to "come back with an army, to straighten things up." And a few weeks before leaving, he asks Art how hard it is to build an atomic bomb. His plan is to throw it at New Orleans "to clean things up." Luckily, the day afterwards he has come to the conclusion that the Bible forbids the use of atomic bombs as it says that one is not allowed to kill "many people by one single blow." That covers weapons of mass destruction, including atomic bombs for John, so he drops his plan of bombing New Orleans for now.

Foreign but Nationalist

Of those having served, the only one who thinks clearly, but still supports the current U.S. administration is Garry Mora— again a person with a questionable claim of really being member of the U.S. nation.

However, Garry Mora did become a U.S. citizen by fighting in the American military. Nevertheless, his take on the current war is that it is wrong. Although Garry is a Democrat, he draws the conclusion that Bush has to be re-elected, so he can "clean up the mess" he would otherwise leave behind. Adam Smith thought that agriculture was the only way to make a profit (Smith 1999), but Garry disagrees. He thinks that there is no way that one can make any money on agriculture at all, and therefore the ARMY should move in and take over all farm land across the country and grow it themselves.

U.S. American Nationalist

It is a third group, in reality a lot smaller than the group of Anglos critical of the U.S., for which Douglas is most well-known. Through the writings of Miller (2000) and the more recent cases of small scale border vigilante groups close to Douglas, that have managed to receive national media attention, a group of white U.S. nationalists has become a main characterization of Douglas throughout the U.S.

But why did they get this way? Let us look how the people at the local gun shop present their case.

One morning while I am at the gun shop (see also — "Fascists at the gun shop", p. 37), Bob comes in while I am talking to Garst. This morning he wants to tell me why he needs to have guns around. "If someone breaks into your house, what you gonna do?" he starts out. His point is that "the police won't protect you. You need to protect yourself." He goes on talking about it for a while, but it seems like most of what he says are NRA catch phrases copied right out of Michael Moore's *Bowling for Columbine*. Although he might talk to me in the believe that he is talking to a European liberal, I receive many other reports about him from other informants that mirror what he has said to me. During another visit, he confirms this to be his analysis, and takes it further, saying that it is a view supported by the Supreme Court, which has ruled that "the police department has no duty to protect any individual in particular."

Another time, Bob gives me some of the background for why his faith in the country's leadership is so low, when he tells me:

> You are supposed to fight for your country and die for your country and then you can get to take part in the glory of your country. And I have fought for my country, and I'm soon going to die for my country, so now it's time for me to take part in some of the glory of my country.

Obviously, this is not happening for him. Maybe because of this, he analyzes the country's leadership:

> You don't destroy the foundation of the pyramid when you sit on top of it [...] But some people are just compelled to do that. [...] The best thing to do is to kill these people. Get rid of the disease. [...] You need to do an operation on society, cut off the bad part.

The Timothy McVeigh case is of particular importance for him, whenever he talks about these things, and he thinks the FBI's handling of the case shows that "some of them [the federal government] just get too full of themselves [...] the thing is just to weed them out."

At the same time, he has no problem with supporting the federal government's war efforts in Iraq:

> Now do you wanna have the war here or there? [...] Screw the United Nations, screw NATO, screw the Middle East and screw the Saudi government. [...] When it comes down to it, it's us or them.

All the passages show how on one hand, Bob views the nation as an organic whole, at the same time as he sees some groups within this nation working against the rest. That is why he needs to defend himself and his country, although he really 'deserves' to be treated better. Bob continues:

> This country is founded upon you that you can do whatever the hell you wanna do. [...] I have the right to not run away from you when you come in here for a hold up. [...] I have the right to stop you right up to the point of killing you.

Partially this might be due to foreign influence, as he describes the last time I visit them: "You know the Comintern? [...] They used to be funding everything here, like SDS[3], groups here and there...." According to Bob, it is due to the lasting influence of the Comintern that Michael Moore is popular today. The communist threat is something that they both believe was and is a really potential problem for the United States. In particular, Bob is proud of the deportation of the IWW organized workers from Bisbee and Douglas in 1917 (see also p. 143), as "those were an absolutely communist organ; they were disrupting the war effort."

Another time, the two of them tell me about their contingency plan:

---

[3]Students for a Democratic Society is the group that Joe had been connected to.

> If they think they can do anything with us, they will feel that there are some of us, and I am not the only one, who ain't gonna let that happen. [...] Then what will they do? If they send the sheriff, I'll shoot the sheriff. If they send the state troops, I'll start shooting them [...] And there are many of us. [...] We're not at the point yet, but they better watch out.

Bob tells me in particular: "Now you may be able to take me down, but you might die in the process." According to more than one source, Bob was shot in the jaw during the Vietnam War.

Do soldiers have the same function as proletarians?

As we have seen, the views on whether the state should be able to take away property differ quite a bit. Both John and Garry do not see private property as God-given, probably due to their experience with prison and war. Bob and others from the far right see it as very important, while Edwin, Peter and Todd do not talk about it much at all. Yet for the entire Douglas cultural elite and Joe, the wars the U.S. have been involved in have nothing to do with the interests of the United States population. And in reality, whenever wars are not about defending the country's territory, they are about taking away or destroying the property/land of foreign people.

Furthermore, most of the those who have been in the military feel cheated by the state, and while all agree that the government is working against their will and interests, they come to different conclusions: the gun shop people turn 'fascist', as Todd calls it, while the cultural elite turn 'liberal' as Bob would say.

The Douglas youth, whether supporting the current war or not, are in a somewhat different position, because they have to choose between joining the military, thereby securing their status as proletarians in Marx's ideological class structure at the lowest end, or not joining and risking access to college due to financial lack, drifting off into Marx's lumpenproletariat.

Generally two approaches have grown out of Marx theory of rebellion: one looking at why proletarians do not rebel, and another looking at why rebellions occur in less developed countries (Boswell and Dixon 1993). Douglas is part of the most developed country of them all, and the number of proletarians is not very high any more. Some of the retirees might have been proletarians once, but the youth generally do not have a long-term future as proletarians in front of them.

However, if one takes it as given that the current wars that the U.S. is involved in are fought for oil that once captured will be exported by some of the major oil companies that are closely linked to the government, their position as soldiers is equals equivalent to workers: The government/company invests in raw material in the form of ammunition, in machinery in the form of tanks, airplanes, and destroyers, and in variable capital in the form of soldiers. If the amount invested in these three categories is lower than the value of the oil on the market, the margin would constitute a profit for the government/company involved, and the soldier would be the exploited worker. In this perspective, the situation very much fits into Marx's model of exploitation and class struggle. (Boswell and Dixon 1993, 681)

Nevertheless, both the youth and the pensioners only speak about their positions; none actually start a struggle for the overthrow of the national elite with a repertoire broader than electoral politics or the personal choice not to join the military. However, there is a fair amount of violence against the laws of the state as we have seen. This kind of 'rebellion' is something the state can endure for quite a long time, and it's something other than a revolution, which is an actual attempt to overthrow the system or the government and which occurs only during short historic moments. However, often revolutions can be the peak of a longer period of rebellious build-up. (Boswell and Dixon 1993, 681)

Such an argument is often used by revisionist historians in their analysis of the Russian revolution point to the increasing levels of violence and cooperation between workers in the years leading up to 1917. They argue that the 1917 revolution was not just a mere coincidence due to very unusual circumstances in that year, but was preceded by an ever increasing number of strikes. (Acton 1990)

Similarly, the situation in Douglas might be a situation of disillusionment and increasing levels of violence, with a revolutionary attempt, such as outlined by the gun shop owners, some time in the future.

On the other hand, the attempts of planning of violent revolution by the gun shop owners are smiled upon by most others I meet. Maria notes that the military is "way too strong" and Zack has similar ideas, as our nightly talk (see — "The Confession", p. 86) reveals, which happened to also be about Zack's spirituality:

I am invited into his room at the Lerman, and he starts talking, while I am offered a soda. He believes that it was the Devil that had asked him to go to Mexico the night before. And that the healing that he has gone through now will mean that he is healed from the Devil. He also tells me how he has been sitting in prison and everyone said that he would never get out, but he had faith and so when he got to speak to the judge he told him that he had faith in the Lord and that he only needed to get out and get his drug problem under control. And Jesus helped him and he did get out on probation. He then reads me a part of a letter that he wants to send to his brother who is in prison for twelve years: "... You have to labor for the Lord and you will find salvation ... " Zack explains: "See, you can't just go and say that it's all unfair to you. You have to labor to be worthy of Gods love, and then He will pay for it."

I argue that perhaps it is actually the system that is unfair, and might it not simply be unfair to him and his brother to be stuck in the situation they are? Zack agrees, that there is that possibility, "but so what? What can you do about it?"

And also, there is the question of the goals of those overthrowing the government would have. The gun shop people would like an overthrow of the elite in order to get rid of foreign elements, and build a society based on raw force. This is what Bob describes as his ideal society, in which "you wouldn't have locks on anything [...] but from when you're about ten years old, you would be shot if you took something that's not yours." While the El Espejo people, although much less vocal about the subject, favor a drastic change that would end the exploitative nature that the U.S. elite has towards other countries. Just because they share an enemy, their goals do not converge, and the current state of affairs might therefore go on indefinitely, or a revolution lead by the gun shop people might start with the burning of all books from the library and the execution of the Douglas cultural elite..

Bruce even says "this is the kind of place where a counter-revolution would find its roots."

But what chance do the cultural elite and the gun shop people have of growing? For most of the high school graduates, the existence of a common national interest is the most obvious, probably because they have recently been closer to the state compared to most others through their schooling, and also because the promised armed forces salary seems to make their own material interests and nationalist ideology merge.

And also among the elderly opinions among vary. While Garry and the gun shop people think that there is such a thing as a national common interest of fundamentally restructuring everything, the others largely do not. For these, one can say that they see it more as a struggle of classes, or at least a struggle of people with differing interests or opinions. But even Garry, Bob and Garst do not agree on what the dysfunctional behavior of this nation as a community is; for Garst and Bob, it is the top that is rotten, while for Garry, it is something that can be fixed from the top by changing the dysfunctional structure of society.

And then there is John who observes that it would not hurt him if San Diego were to be invaded, because he has no family there. While at the same time he favors cleaning up "the mess" in various city administrations or branches of the military. This kind of unstructured wish of a rebellion against all the 'evil forces' within the state by using the 'good parts' of the state is probably also held by quite a lot.

Chapter 6

Douglas and the World

P HYSICALLY, Douglas is of course both part of the world and part of the United States, just as any other town that is geographically located within the United States. However, as we have seen, the borders of the United States are not synchronized with the imagined boundaries of a system of production and consumption. Moreover, although most understand that rights and values are unevenly distributed across the globe, it is not the nation but instead the close proximity to the border that defines the special possibilities that are open to many of the Douglasites, with the country being mainly responsible for those opportunities (and for some the exploitation) that exist within law enforcement.

Nevertheless, Douglasites categorize Douglas as part of the U.S. on a cognitive, indirect level. Even those that specify that they see Douglas as in some way not part of the United States also relate to this way of thinking.

This is different from the discussions about nationalism, because it shows how Douglasites define Douglas' relation to the U.S. without talking in direct nationalist or anti-nationalist terms.

Douglas connected to the United States

One thing that helps me understand how people believe that Douglas is part of the United States is through the comparisons they make with other places in the United States:

Connection through comparability

One prominent example of such a comparison comes up some months into John's stay in Douglas when he tells me that he wants to leave for New York, because he has never seen it before and he would like to go watch a Yankees game[1]. I help him find an airplane ticket on the net. The only friend that I have ever seen show up at his apartment, advises him, "friends you make in Douglas are friends you make for life. Go to New York and watch your [Yankee] game, but then come back," when I visit John to ask him to come to the library for his good-bye party (see also — "John's good-bye reception", p. 38).

John plans to buy a car for the trip. He finds a map of New York and he starts wondering which route he is will take so that he can avoid the road tax over the bridges to and from Manhattan, since he expects that he will have to cross many bridges to commute to the job he is planning to get. "Maybe you should try to use the underground instead," I suggest. He had no idea there was such a thing as a subway. I show him the web page and write down a web address for him to access and get a special senior citizen discount card for the NYC Transit system.

After John arrives in New York he sends me occasional e-mails for a while. The last mail I get from him is:

> I am planning on leaving (NEW YORK CITY) in the next few days. Most likely on the 3rd of July, I will arrange a flight to San Diego, Ca., which will get me there in time for the 4th of July parade in Coronado. [... New York]'s pretty much of a boring place with a lot of poverty much like Douglas. GOD BLESS YOU JOHN

I tell Sarah about the e-mail while we drive around Douglas. "Where has he been in New York?" she asks, indicating that she finds the comparison absurd.

---

[1] The New York Yankees are a famous baseball team.

John is not the only one who draws the connection between NYC and Douglas. Luke is a student at Cochise College who often reads at the library. He has a father from Arkansas and a mother from the neighboring Mexican state of Sonora. He grew up in Arkansas and only came to Douglas recently with his mother. One time tells me: "See, Douglas is a lot like New York with everything close by in the city center ['everything' being the library, the Grand, the Lerman and a few dollar stores]. While Bisbee is like L.A. with everything spread out all over the place. That is why I like Douglas a lot better."

And this is only one of the different ways that Douglasites connect their town with the United States. Although the comment made by the friend about "friends in Douglas" differentiates Douglas from New York, it also compares the two as if they are the same size. John's e-mail from New York connects them even more directly. John also places Douglas culturally within the United States, when he expects a table outside the library, Art and me have placed there as part of his good-bye reception, to be a fundraiser. This must be based on his experience that fundraisers are quite common throughout the United States. Given the unemployment rate and poverty, it does not really apply to Douglas, especially not to events held on the library parking lot. The only fundraiser I ever hear about during my time in Douglas is a Democratic picnic out on the other side of Bisbee. John is not considering the local context, but is instead solemnly relying on national cultural standards.

There is not always consensus about how other places relate to Douglas. For example, Jeff talks about Tucson as merely an "extension of Douglas". I try to point that out when I speak to the youngsters around the Hotel in Tucson where Robert works, but in their view Douglas is a very different place because it is very small and rural, although the girls from Douglas are supposed to be the prettiest in the state of Arizona. Bruce, who also holds that "when only you go as far as Tucson you come into a whole 'nother world", also mirrors this opinion.

However, all these comparisons, regardless of the similarities or differences, place Douglas as just another city inside the United States. The comparisons also show that it is unclear to them what life actually is like in other cities.

Connection through interdependence

Another way to place Douglas inside the United States is by looking at how the decisions made in Douglas affect the entire country.

One example of this is delivered by Art. After I help him release his web page on his self-constructed telescope (see p. 200), he starts considering the idea of publishing more web pages on various topics he has studied over the years. One of the ideas he has is to make a page on an idea that he has about producing engines that can run on "coal slurry" as replacement for oil[2]. But Art's main concern is the effect it will have on the world if he releases the information on a web page. "We might just have another black Friday," Art contemplates, "and we know who will lose the most in times of economic crisis — those that are at the bottom already." After thinking about it, Art decides not to release the information, and instead his second page is on a new kind of windmill that works by letting a glider airplane drag a cable back and forth. Art thinks that it will change the economy at a slower rate, and that he might actually get some help from some of the oil companies, because they will not understand the importance of his work. In the end, Art's invention will mean that oil will lose its value, and thereby all wars in the Middle East will end, according to his thinking. "Oil is through!" is what he writes me in an e-mail a few weeks after I have left the first time.

And this is only one example of how many see Douglas at the very center of national debates, and the peripheral nature that I attribute to Douglas' geographic location does not exist in the same way for many.

Photo: Johannes Wilm

Picture 16: Shopping opportunities in Douglas are limited.

Douglas disconnected from the United States

On the other hand, there are those who try to show how Douglas is disconnected from the rest of the United States.

Maria makes contact with me the first time when she speaks to me at the library and invites me to come with some friends to go to Sierra Vista the next day. Kevin describes Sierra Vista as exemplifying "everything that is wrong with this country." It is a town based around an ARMY base with large roads and branches of all the major store and restaurant chains, and it has absolutely no unique personality. The Douglas kids love to go there though, because it is the closest English-speaking town that is large enough

---

[2]Art thinks that it should be possible to grind up coal into really tiny particles and then mix them with water — a mix that he terms "coal slurry". A modification is required to a diesel engine, which he explains to me for about an hour, and as a result should make motors run just as effectively. One of the main points of his idea is that the particles will get into the engine in different places based on their size. This fuel will not work for gasoline-powered engines unless they are converted to run on diesel fuel.

to have a mall. Although Agua Prieta has a mall, the youths have a valid justification — it does not have any English bookstore or CD store. The youths and Kevin agree that Sierra Vista is much more part of the United States than Douglas is — they just have different views on whether that is positive or negative.

Another example is Lou, at the Douglas Historic Society, who grew up in Douglas but then moved away until just a few years ago, when he came back as a senior citizen. One of his main points is that "Douglas is connected to the [Mexican] peso economy," meaning that the economy of Douglas goes up and down depending on how the peso does, rather than the USD. This has to do with the fact that Douglas has very few production facilities itself and is therefore just about completely dependent upon Mexican workers consumer goods at American stores. As the guide on my winter visitor tour of Agua Prieta says: "When I think about what they mean for our economy, I don't mind that I have to wait so long to check out those huge amounts of things at Food City when I'm waiting behind them in the line."

Another way of mentally disconnecting Douglas from the United States can be found in the cultural domain. Once, the Barkers and I are invited to Lisa's graduation party because we are part of the neighborhood and there are family connections between Lisa and Bill, who is Sarah's employee. We do not ever receive an official invitation, so Bruce's father refuses to come. While I had no idea that such an occasion would require an invitation, Bruce thinks it is just a minor cultural difference that he wants to be flexible about, and Sarah agrees to come along on that basis but she feels uncomfortable about it. Another question is the gift that Sarah thinks is appropriate to give in this situation. I volunteer to call Maria's mother earlier that day to find out what the cultural norm is in Douglas. The mother is not home, but Maria informs me that it is one gift per family and that it should stay within a few dollars. Sarah ends up buying an alarm clock, and I am the only one of the three of us who watches the unwrapping of the gift later on; the alarm clock was apparently not quite in the price range for people living in this part of town.

Here the American Barkers are clearly just as foreign to the cultural norm of Douglas as I am. As we have seen, this foreignness is probably the exact reason why they like Douglas.

Agents from the outside

A concern that I meet often is the question of whether people are really who they say they are, or whether they are just "pretending" while they really are agents who are allied to an outside force.

When I tell Todd and Kevin that Bruce is trying to apply for a job with Voice of America (VoA)[3], Todd says: "You know what you need to get in there, right? Good contacts to the CIA!" Kevin seems to agree. It is unclear though whether they mean that Bruce really is a CIA agent, or whether they are implying that he does not have a chance. Bruce himself remarks on Todd having lived in Columbia, and that U.S. citizens would only live there for a long time if they were CIA agents. At the same time, both Todd and Bruce are certain that Kevin has contacts deep into the local drug business, but I do not recall them having mentioned him as a CIA-agent. Edwin talks about "two CIA agents staying at the Grand [permanently]" he has heard about. "You know they are supposed not to operate inside the country, but they never kept to that," he explains. Todd remarks: "Edwin was probably himself involved with the cops when he was running his drug store...giving them names and stuff."

At one point in time, I myself suspect John of being a possible agent, when he shows signs of being able to differentiate between reality and fantasy in his conversations. And when I ask him whether he has ever been working for the CIA or FBI, he answers; "No, but I applied to get in 1974 [approximate year] and as a test they played the video where Kennedy gets shot. I was supposed to take out the hit man, but instead I fired at the President. I did just what Lee Harvey Oswald did; I shot the President."

A few weeks later, Bruce remarks: "And you thought John was the agent!" when he starts suspecting Art of being one. At the time, Bruce needs a way to transmit sound from his mini disc player over the phone line because he is applying for a job as a stringer in Nigeria, and he will have to send his interviews to a media center in London, in addition he will also need a good

---

[3]VoA is the U.S.'s foreign news broadcast.

microphone for interviews. It is June when he is looking closer into the matter, and first he plans to buy an expensive interface and microphone in Tucson. Before he leaves, we go by the library together and while Bruce talks at the counter, I ask Art whether he knows anything about microphones and sound equipment. Art is somehow an expert on sound and microphone. He tells us how one can build a 't-pad' out of a few resistors to connect something to the phone line and he seems to have intimate knowledge of the routines phone companies employ in order to detect bugs on the phone line and how to build equipment that circumvents that. Then he talks about the microphone: "You want to get an electret mike, they are always way better than all the others." Art goes on to describe how to build various parabolas to collect different amounts of sound, with or without the knowledge of person being recorded. Then he suddenly remembers that he has one of those microphones lying in his car, and he offers to sell it to Bruce. When we see it the next day, it appears tiny, but when we try it out it can record absolutely everything within a 20m radius. Art sells it for 10 USD and he helps me to figure out the best way to build the t-pad that is exactly right for Bruce's Minidisc. But even though we add a piece from the board of an old photocopy machine that Art has located in a yard behind the Lerman, the signal strength is too low. "How does he know this stuff?" Bruce wonders, "never again will I say he is crazy!" A little while later, Bruce gets the idea of Art being a possible agent: "His explanation that he liked to play music when he was in high school just doesn't cut it. You know, where do you think he has those Zionist ideas about Israel from? [...] And you know what they do with those they don't need anymore, they just dump them — if they don't kill them." Bruce is implying that Art is in Douglas in order to hide from the CIA or another secret service that he was employed by. The next day or so, when I ask Art how he knows about these things, he answers evasively that it is very easy. When I then ask him whether he ever has been employed to build surveillance equipment, he merely answers: "Several mobsters tried to hire me to do it."

On one of the last days I am in Douglas, Art asks me whether I have heard Sun William speak Polish on his cell phone. Sun William is a man in his fifties who walks up and down the streets of Douglas with a shopping cart. In the summer he walks around without a shirt, and in the winter he has his cart and clothing decorated with Christmas attire. Every few minutes he yells "darliiiing, darliiiing," and he tells me he is looking for his girl who is "around here somewhere." Sun William is seen as crazy by absolutely everyone else, but according to Art, it is all just pretension. "He probably is really rich and just wants to hide it away, so he acts real crazy," Art says, "I was walking behind him yesterday when he suddenly pulled out his cell phone and started speaking in Polish and had a real long unintelligible conversation." On my second trip to Douglas, Sun William does not remember me, and I see him the first time when he is sitting at the Grand cafeteria. As I walk in from the hotel side, I assume that he believes that I am only a short time visitor. And for the first time, William actually speaks intelligibly. He asks me where I am from, and to my surprise he speaks fluent German. His story is that he has been living in Berlin and parts of West Germany for several years, working for Mercedes. "I really like the U.S. more, but it was a mistake coming back, it is hard to find a place to live here," he explains. I see him for the next few weeks, but never talk to him again much until the morning when I am to leave. This time, I ask about his name "Mahmoud," as he had told me at the Grand, and whether that is Mexican, as most I talk to expect him to be Mexican due to his dark skin complexion. "No, Palestinian," he explains — and then he does not say much more other than that he has been living in Douglas for quite some time and moves back on forth across the border frequently.

After I have talked to the people at the gun shop the first time, Mr. Fernandez takes me aside that evening. He tells me: "You know, this is a secret, but they are really police agents." According to Mr. Fernandez, they really do not hold the views they portray and were just placed there by the police when the vigilante groups started showing up a few years ago.

A few days before I am to leave for the first time, I am stopped by one of the infrequent visitors of the library. Although I have not seen him for months, he knows exactly when my plane leaves. And he is also certain what the entire purpose of my stay in Douglas was: "I know you are studying to become a CIA-agent." And although I refute it, he is sure of his theory, and so he yells down the street, as

Photo: Johannes Wilm

Picture 17: Border Patrol trying to recruit youngsters with an information booth

I try to make my exit: "I won't tell anybody, honestly!"

The number of alleged agents is certainly higher than any other place I have come across.

Law Enforcement

Besides the agents who may or may not be real, there are the officers who clearly do exist and can be seen as intruders as the following episode will exemplify.

One evening after a long day at the library a few days after reporting John's gun to the police for the first time, I walk out towards D-Hill from Douglas wearing my headphones and listening to my music at 10pm. Halfway out there, a Border Patrol pulls up from behind and asks me: "Hey, where are you going?" I tell him that I am planning to go to the top of D-Hill so I can to look back at Douglas from there, because it is a magnificent view. The Border Patrol tries to convince me to turn back by telling me that it is very dangerous "to walk out here at night," because there are illegal immigrants crossing all the time. I answer back that "yeah, yeah, I know, that is what they say" and continue walking. The Border Patrol gives up and drives further on. I can see him stop at the foot of D-Hill.

After another 10 minutes, almost simultaneously, three police cars pull up behind me, and two Border Patrols pull up simultaneously from the front. I stand still and turn my music off as the five law enforcement officers surround me. They tell me they need to see my id and documents. I only carry my Arizona Driver License because I am not going to cross the border. But as I tell them I am not a U.S. citizen, they tell me that is insufficient and I need to have my visa on me at all times. Then they go on to tell me that it is very dangerous to walk there and that it is better for me to stay within the city limits at all times. Since I am in the mood of not taking anything from them, I tell them that I am "pretty sure that it is legal to walk out here at night." One of the police officers answers back: "Look man, you don't want to be pulling this it's-my-right shit. You are not a resident here; you are supposed to behave like a guest.... and it takes one second and you are right back in Denmark or wherever the hell you came from." Another police officer adds: "All they," pointing at the Border Patrols, "have to say is that you are interfering with operations by walking out here". After that I decide that the best thing to do is to just answer every statement with "yes, Sir" and after a few minutes of "informing," they offer to drive me back to where I am staying in Douglas. I ask for my driver license, but the police officer tells me I will get it back when I return Douglas. When we pull off, another Border Patrol pulls off the road to talk to the remaining four officers. Back in Douglas, they return my driver license to me.

When I tell the story to the Barkers the next day, they are stunned, and are now even more distrustful of the Border Patrols. The first time that I eat dinner with them while still living at the Lerman, they already are talking about how the border agents have been taking over D-Hill and Bruce in particular is upset that they have put up a gate at the entrance there, even though the hill really is supposed to be used by the school. I also tell Todd, and the news spreads fast. Kevin's reaction is mostly focused on the issue of their legal right to close off an area. "Next thing, they can just close down

G-Avenue, saying they have operations running there," Kevin says, "When these left-wingers talk about the militarization of the border area, they really have a point there." Shortly before I leave, Edwin talks to an FBI contact of his, and the agent informs him that they had received a wire stating that European nationals are being hired by Al Qaida to poison the water supply, and the Douglas water supply is located on the road towards D-Hill. Edwin thinks that is too ridiculous a reason, so he decides not to tell me — I find out about it through Todd and Sarah, and Edwin then verifies it when I ask him.

Hiding from the government

As the last episode shows, there are many suspicious feelings towards the government among many Douglasites. Most of those suspicious of the government have not actually been in conflict with the government or any of its agents. But there are also a number of more extreme examples. One of those is Joe.

Joe used to be a student activist in the Ann Arbor, Michigan area during the Vietnam War and was indicted for conspiring to blow up a federal building back there. But then the government dropped all charges and let him go. He proudly shows me the 350 pages of his FBI file that the government released under the 'Freedom of Information Act' a few years ago. After his trial, he moved out to the Arizona desert where he has been building an environmentally sustainable house that was initially planned for a commune.

Until he gets involved with the ecological program, he had been trying to cut himself off from the government as much as possible. After 9/11, a few people in a government vehicle came out to him allegedly in order to ask about the road, but Joe was sure that they really only wanted to map his property. He refused to let them give him an address, so he has to drive down to a small village quite far away, in order to check his mail.

Even though the environmental project is government sponsored, he is still very nervous about the government. Once, while the two of us are putting up fences for keeping cattle out of his property, there is a low flying bomber passing over his property.

Photo: Johannes Wilm

Picture 18: Joe's self built house is energy efficient and not connected to the main grid.

Joe remarks, although with a sarcastic undertone, that they might just be out to finish him off this time.

Conclusion

As we have seen, Douglas is definable both as part of the United States and as standing apart from it in many ways. To a certain extent, it seems that each individual defines Douglas in his or her own way and that definition is connected to the overall view one has of U.S. society and government, whether as a positive thing that is worth protecting or a negative thing that he or she needs to disconnect from as much as possible.

People like Joe are clearly hiding in order to be as isolated as possible, and at first I thought I saw the outlines of an idea similar to that presented by Miller (2000), with Douglas being a separate space of its own, disconnected from any world system. However, if we look closer at the examples at hand, we discover that Douglas is more closely connected to a world system. In the case of the teenagers and Kevin seeing Sierra Vista as being a completely different place, and the Barkers feeling like they culturally are foreigners, Douglas is simply seen as having a heavier influx of Mexican culture, and not just being an isolated sphere. In the case of the conjectures about the presence of government agents, it is largely the people who presume to see these agents who also have a global view of the world that includes the United States just being one major actor. In the case of Joe hiding from the government, he starts out with a socialist world system perspective, and the United States is the only power that he has to concentrate on, given its current geopolitical position.

The fact that Douglas is largely still seen as being part of the United States is interesting, due to the huge influx of people with a non-U.S.-national (mostly Mexican) background, which has been part of Douglas's life for many decades at a level that many other areas are only experiencing in the most recent phase of hyper-globalization. Somehow, there is a striking influence of American homogenized culture that far outweighs the size of the 'gringo' part of the population.

The phenomenon is not a new one. Looking once more at Marx's dual notion of capitalism, at one point in time he sees the high influx of foreign ideas, money and people that occur under capitalism, which leads to a homogenization of all countries involved, and at another time he notices the strength that nationalist ideology can develop in a capitalist society. While Marx changes his perception when he notices the latter, the two tendencies exist at the very same time in the same society (see also p. 212).

So who are the Douglasites really? — Concluding Remarks

AS we have seen, there are a number of different communities that are present in Douglas simultaneously. The same person is a member of several of these, depending on what factors one looks at. For example, Soerlie fits very well into the local way of dealing with crime, at the same time that he is both participating in and has an understanding of a network of production and consumption that has a somewhat different scale. If we look at the geographic extent of the communities, rather than what they consist of, we can find three different communities present in Douglas:

- *A global community* — of interdependence in terms of consumption and production. That does not mean that everybody consumes the same amount or produces the same things, but rather that there is a global interdependence in terms of these two factors.

- *A national community* — built upon the opportunities that jobs in the military and other law enforcement can give.

- *A local community* — which is based on the number of possibilities by which the specific geographic location of Douglas makes it possible to circumvent the law, and which creates a community in terms of what the state would call 'illegal' activity.

Now all of these are grounded on economic factors, but the individual strategies for obtaining and spending money vary widely, and so do the strengths of the various communities among the various individuals.

We can therefore conclude, at least in the case of Douglas, that there is no such thing as a single community that monopolizes one geographic space — neither for the entire town nor for a single individual. It is very important to be able to observe them in these times of crisis when the national allegiance of people with several possible identities tends to be under open attack — the unemployed, the migrant workers, or any other subgroup that the ruling elite can blame for the current problems facing the economy.

But mental categories do not tell us all that much, if they are not connected to anything that has an impact on the way people live. Let us therefore look at some of the other, more materialistic, things we found:

Class

At this stage, where capitalism based on private capital seems to have left large parts of the population outside its grasp, clear-cut distinctions following a Marxist class model are hard to spot. Also, communication is largely unhindered by economic distinctions in Douglas, where the property owning class is mostly absent. Nevertheless, economic distinctions exist among the Douglasites, but there are different ways in which individuals handle them.

For example, January, the child of two Mexican doctors, decides to ignore her position in the economic situation. And together with her psychologist child boyfriend Jeff, in her general theory of society she is ignoring the fact that there is no such thing as a capitalist economic system independent of a state. One does not need to have read Marx (1999) in order to understand that the state, with its military and police force, protects property relations and therefore assures the individual capitalist's control over the means of production that are out of his personal reach and that otherwise would be in the sole control of the employed workers. Also, they ignore the fact that an employed person will always get less than

Photo: Johannes Wilm

Picture 19: Luis hopes he has found life-time job in the Douglas fire brigade.

what his work is worth in order to create a profit for a person who is sitting higher in the chain of command.

January's idea of wanting "to work hard" seems to be in line with the Protestant ethic of work. But she and Jeff do not speak in this way all the time. One night, when she first explains her family situation to me, her emphasis veers more towards the problems of being economically dependent on one's parents and explaining the Danish and Scandinavian student stipend system, she exclaims that it is a lot nicer to be "dependent on the government instead of one's parents." Jeff tells me in a debate about social democracy that he has "much less problems with tax increases than [he] do[es] with all the liberal social agendas."

Whether these are small glimpses of their true views, while they hide them away at other times, I do not know. I only observe that they are inconsistent, but both agree that January's parents are losers in the current economic system, while Jeff's father is a winner because he is a psychologist who can afford a pool.

Photo: Johannes Wilm

Picture 20: Returning soldiers from Iraq during a parade

Jacob Holdt (1979, 132–133), looking at various American sub-groups during the 1970s, before Fox News ever entered the media scene, made a similar observation; the degree of one's desperation seems to have little influence over the stubbornness with which many middle class kids defend the ideology that in the United States anyone can become a millionaire, if only he works hard. Holdt differentiates between middle and upper class, because it is the middle class that believes in this ideology the strongest. However, Holdt also falls short of offering an explanation for this phenomenon.

The Importance of Structure

Jeff is probably the one informant who is most vocal about his doubts that the conditions under which some people have to live are due to the current structure of society rather than an effect of nothing but their own actions. I am sure he is not alone with his view and it is therefore a relevant point to discuss, although it must be noted that the "Douglas Cultural Elite" does not agree with this view at all.

In order to see the importance of society's structure in this situation, let us look at the particular reason why people like Zack, Peter and John exist in Douglas in the way they do. Of course, each one of them has had a great part in deciding upon their own particular lifestyle and what activities they want to engage in. Their own position, which they and others probably see as being undesirable, might be a result largely of their own particular choices. However, such an explanation is inadequate to explain why there is a whole culture of lumpenproletariat (see — "The term 'lumpenproletariat'", p. 214) in the United States, consisting of poor people, but not poor enough to starve — at least not quite yet. In order to be able to explain this, one has to look outside the scope of an individual informant and instead focus on the place within and the structure of the society he is a part of. Now this is not to say that this structure has any particular purpose or is self-sustaining, as some structuralists or functionalists would have it; the structure can be in constant development and has therefore to be understood in the context of one particular time.

This is where the oil crisis (Berthoud and Sabelli 1979), the falling profit rate (Brenner 2002) and the elites' reaction to it all (Neale 2004) as well as the subsequent overproduction crisis come in: these events created the current massive amount of lumpenproletariat. To a great measure, the presence of a lumpenproletariat at the global level probably also explains the presence of a lumpenproletariat in the United States, because a higher overall rate of lumpenproletariat in the world will likely also have its effect on the United States.

The second part of the structural setting, which concerns the presence of various sources of funding for the lumpenproletariat in the United States, might also be seen as a particular historical feature, because the end of social welfare programs, in particular social security, are seen by many Douglasites as a looming danger that might end up sending millions into starvation and onto the streets.

A prophetic value?

First of all, immigration into the United States from Mexico does exist, and Spanish is spreading quickly all across the country, as Huntington (2004) points out. But while the areas in which Spanish is spoken today are usually those with many manual labor jobs, and the interaction between English and Spanish speakers is a rather recent phenomenon due to immigration, in Douglas the interaction has existed for at least a hundred years. Douglas has gone through various schemes of social organization at different times before arriving at the very low employment rate that exists now. Douglas can therefore be seen as a model of how ethnic relations will be in much of the country in future generations.

Social stratification

Another conclusion we can extract from the study of Douglas is that ethnicity in the end has little relevance. None of my Anglo informants are in any position of power due to their ethnic background. That does not mean that people are not aware of who belongs to which ethnic group, and when I am taken for being John's son by a local Hispanic man (see p. 191) and he figures out that I am indeed from Europe, his immediate reaction is: "Oh, I thought you were white." It shows that people differentiate along those lines, but as we have seen in numerous places, the distinction does not make a lot of difference in practical matters. Partially it might be because the social and political power of the overwhelming numbers of Hispanics in Douglas has suppressed the discriminatory practices of the prejudicial parts of the White/Anglo population, but also stratification the other way round, with Hispanics on top and Whites at the bottom, does not happen very much. Despite more recent theories that try to look at categories of social stratification other than social class, the old Marxist models seem to be the most fruitful. During the part of Douglas' history when segregation was based on ethnicity, it was a place with lots of jobs and the race distinction was actively employed by the company in order to keep management and blue-collar workers apart. The total lack of jobs for vast proportions of the population, and consequently the prevalence of the lumpenproletariat, then had the effect that the stratification along ethnic lines was eliminated.

Along with Marx's 150 year old analysis of the lumpenproletariat being an uncertain and unpredictable group, which still seems applicable, Anderson's 80 year old description of the distinctively American hobo also seems to be close to the reality of many people in Douglas: although many are economically poor, quite a few of them are relatively well read and following what is going on — rather than just being drugged down and rather stupid people as one might believe if one accepted the current TV news.

The times, they are changing?

If things are still the same as they have been for the last 150 years, then the utopia that Art and others wait for is something that will always be in the far future and the Armageddon that the U.S. is steering towards in the view of many informants is nothing but a consistent belief among a fringe segment of the population. One could argue against this claim, that indeed, things have changed, because the U.S. is in a completely different situation. While the hobos described by Anderson are urbanized, and try to escape the kinds of permanent attachments that the rural life gives (Anderson 1923), the Douglasites instead seem like stranded characters who have given up on the world and try to make the best of their situations. Art shows it most clearly, when he starts reading Jack Kerouac's *On the Road*, a classic on the free life of some youngsters, who travel back and forth across the country. "It's not how I remembered it," he says, when returning it to the library after only a few days. He has just moved out of the car and into the Lerman Hotel, which is his first relatively permanent stay for a long time. He even goes so far as to tell me that I will probably find him there if I return to Douglas "in a decade or so."

That is not to say, that their revolutionary spirit is any less true, but utopia is simply no longer seen as a certain thing that will come with necessity. For John, the "straightening up," that the country has to do is even a repetitive event.

Action?

Nevertheless, the most important information we can get out of this study is how and what kind of action one can take. Constantly high unemployment figures can tell us, that an organization of the lumpenproletariat is necessary in the planning of a world revolution or some more localized struggle for a democratic and economically just society. Otherwise, the ruling class can control the proletariat much too easily by using members of the lumpenproletariat as strikebreakers. Engels' and Marx's discomfort with the lumpenproletariat, although understandable, has to be left behind if social change is the ultimate goal.

Problems

The problems connected with this task seem to be many-fold. One problem is with those like Maria, who are bright enough to have understood much of the power structure of society by themselves and young enough to be recruited as organizers, because they are also the ones who are still interesting for the occasional employers, as the example with Wal-Mart shows.

Just before Christmas, when Maria is close to getting fired, and she can already see the pressure that is building up on her, I suggest that she try to join a union, preferably the IWW, but the little hope she has for keeping her job and finally getting health insurance gives her enough incentive to prevent her from taking the risk of upsetting the company further by joining a union.

Another problem is the cultural factor. As we have seen in the chapter on border crossings, it is only a few who are allowed to cross the cultural border, and it is not one single border, but a whole range of borders with many sub-groups in between pure Anglos and pure Mexicans. Not knowing the things that are considered "cool" by a target group severely hinders the possibility of communicating the necessity for organization.

The problem of communicating seems less severe with those over thirty years of age, and it decreases further for those even older, as my communication with Zack, Mr. Fernandez as well as all the older Anglos show.

A third problem is the extent to which those youngsters who are second generation academics, like Jeff and January, can turn very conservative and take the myth of the American Dream seriously. Although these people could play a fundamental role in reshaping society, the need to differentiate himself or herself from everyone else seems to be a major factor in turning them into agents of conservatism. However, it is too early to tell whether my agitation will have any long-term consequences on this group.

A fourth problem is presented by the chapter on money (see p. 45). In comparison to the conditions described by Anderson (1923), the amount of Marxist or anarchist literature read by the members of the lumpenproletariat seems quite low, and is often replaced by the Bible, Adam Smith or, in the case of the cultural elite, various critics who are looking at single issues. This means that agitation has to start from the very beginning.

A fifth problem is the factor that some of those who are dissatisfied go to the extreme right; although the gun shop people are revolutionary and have much of the same understanding of the basic facts, their conclusion turns them to something that closely resembles fascism. Just ignoring them, or declaring them as the main enemy as leftists have done traditionally, cannot work if they grow in numbers. What has to be done is to develop a widely applicable psychological strategy to win over people with a background of "serving the nation."

Positive factors

But aside from these problems, which need to be overcome somehow, there are a number of positive factors to build upon. As the chapter on crime (see p. 119) shows, the high level of crime indicates a general decline in belief in the law. The need to overthrow the government is also quite widespread. However, one has to watch out that it does not lead to corruption within some future movement.

Furthermore, most of those who have returned from a war frequently look for an analysis of society that focuses more on internal conflicts of opinions or interests, although these do not have to follow along class-based ideas of society (see — "War &

Nationalism", p. 145). A greater challenge lies in convincing high school students not to join the Armed Forces, but this task also seems not too difficult, and at the time of writing, the military has missed its recruitment goal for the 3rd consecutive month (Glesne 2005).

Another positive factor is the relatively low degree of ethnic segregation that, as outlined, is partially due to the low employment rate. While ethnic diversity often has been seen as a hindrance to organization, it seems that combined with unemployment, its effect is not as negative. In cases where people are forced to live close together and each person only has access to a part of the things seen as desirable (consumer goods, bits of information, contacts, technological knowledge, language skills, etc.); it actually integrates rather than segregates.

Also, in a border town, knowledge is spread according to a much more heterogeneous pattern, and a group of people cooperating across the various barriers will therefore be likely to build up a great amount of knowledge of how to circumvent the power apparatus of either of the involved states. Just for this, in the planning of a cross-national or global change, towns like Douglas should not be ignored.

Appendix A

People

Mr. Fernandez

Mr. Fernandez is the daytime manager at the Lerman and he stays in number 16.

When I knock on his door on the morning of the day I find the Lerman, Mr. Fernandez comes out. He is an old man looking like he is in his fifties or sixties; he has lost all his front teeth, has white hair and wrinkles mainly under his eyes. I ask him whether any rooms are vacant and he immediately points out that they share showers and toilets. I tell him that I do not care and that I need a place for up to six months. He first shows me #13, which is a smaller room with a view on a dark side alley, but then also offers me #6, which is a lot bigger and its window gives a good view over 11th street. He asks me what work I am doing and I tell him I am a student without a job. "At Cochise College?" he asks (a question I will have to answer again and again throughout my stay in Douglas).

One issue Mr. Fernandez has with me in the early days is that he wants to go to the whorehouse across the line with me and pushes me to go to an office to get condoms for that purpose. He argues: "Why not, it's just like going to the store and buying a piece of meat, there you give her money and you know what you get [laughter]." After I stubbornly refuse to ever go with him to the whorehouse, he brings up a second issue: he wants me to go to church. I do not want to do that either. But after he takes me out for breakfast with

187

him several times to discuss why I need to go to church, I agree
to go to church twice and then after that decide whether I want
to continue. Mr. Fernandez then gives me a Christian magazine
New Man to read. He also tells me that he has been a missionary in
Mexico and that he attends the *Church of God*. He wants me to go
to an English speaking church though, and so a few days later he
makes plans to send me with one of the residents, Zack.

Mr. Fernandez himself speaks English, but none of the other
members of his family who come by seem to be able to, whether
they come from Agua Prieta or Phoenix.

John

John arrives in Douglas on the 22nd of January from Arkansas,
where he grew up. He is in his fifties. His family owns a woodcraft
shop back in Arkansas. There is not much I can be sure of in matters
of his background because some of it just cannot be true and he
has a colorful fantasy. And he is consistent in these stories, so they
are more than just impromptu ideas of his. For example, he tells
the following stories several times, usually when people ask him
which state he is from. However, quite a lot of the information
he presents is backed up by concrete evidence, so I cannot avoid
taking it seriously. It seems quite certain that he has been in the
prison near Douglas between 1991 and 1999. More uncertain is his
relation to Douglas, because he tells me he has been "in and out of
Douglas" since he was about 20.

Other things he says sound rather crazy. For example much of
what he tells me about his mother is evidence that he has a lively
fantasy:

> See when I was young, my mother used to go out danc-
> ing. She would meet up with Bill Clinton and they
> would just go on dancing all night [moving as if he was
> dancing].... Just dancin' and dancin', all night long....
>
> And my father would find his gun and go chase them
> with his pickup ... all over town. He drove around and
> around, all night long. But they'd never be caught. And
> they'd just be dancin' and dancin'.

Another one of his favorites is his story about his family. First he tells me that his grandparents are still in charge of the family property. Now I figure that might actually be technically possible, but then he goes on to say that also his great grandmother is still alive: "She was born in 1875 and is still going strong." And that is not just some minor point for him: "And I can tell my grandparents right now, that if they plan to live that long, it ain't gonna happen!"

At the same time, John seems to be able to distinguish between what others will accept and what they will not as an actual description of reality. When I sit with him and Bruce in 10th Street Park once, I try to lead his imagination to a greater extreme to see how far he will follow me, so I suggest that his family might have paid Bruce's mother to plan an attack against him. He looks at me for a few seconds before he concludes: "You think that might just be my imagination about my family trying to kill me? Well it might just be."

Although John owns a great deal or most of the family property in Arkansas, it is his grandparents who cheat him by paying only a laughable amount for rent on the property they occupy. When they die, he is to inherit the property, but until then he expects them to somehow try to kill him.

In 1991, John had been in New Orleans and wanted to go to San Diego, but John himself best tells the story:

> I wanted to go to San Diego, but I wanted to buy a gun first, so I went down to the police office and asked them whether they would give me a license. They said they wouldn't cause it would look like I would be one of them, but they said I could just go down and get a gun by myself. So I went down and got myself a gun.
>
> [...]
>
> When I was on the interstate, there were all these cars following me all the way from New Orleans and stuff. They'd like pass and then just slow down right in front of me and funky stuff like that.
>
> [...]

> I came up to a motel and the lady there said I could buy myself into a chicken dinner for 4 USD... but then this black dude comes up and talks her into givin' him the chicken dinner and I got whatever the black guy had picked out of some dumpster.
>
> That was it; I had enough. I drove on up onto a bridge and when the black dude came by, I started shooting until the car stopped... then I went on driving down the road and took pot shots at other cars.
>
> When I came to Cochise County, they finally got me
>
> [...]
>
> Part of the case of the state was that I hadn't hurt nobody, so I'd missed them all. But I hit some guy's water bottle, they said.

John tells me this within the first ten minutes after we meet. At first, I am not sure whether to believe him or not. However, a few months later, when I have shown him how to use the Internet at the library, John provides the evidence for having been in prison by finding and printing out his prison records.

After John was released in 1999, he first went to Tucson, where he sat out his probation. Then he went back to his family in Arkansas. When John comes to Douglas this time, he has just had a major fight with his family, which owns a wood shop back in Arkansas. He felt that he had been doing most of the work, while his brother "got all the credit for it" and so he wanted to leave. His father then gave him a pickup truck to take with him.

But before leaving, John decided that he would "smash up everything" he could in the trailer where he was staying and which he only partially owned. He then decided to go to Douglas and drove all the way across the country, but his pickup broke down 20 miles short of Benson[1]. Instead of calling a mechanic, he "smashed all the windows and pulled out the gear stick that [he] recently [had] bought." When I ask him why, he answers "so they won't get nothing when they find it." He then walked to Benson, and there the police gave him a free ticket for the bus to Douglas.

---

[1]Benson is the closest interstate exit for Douglas.

First I do not know whether I should believe this either, but a few weeks later, when John has found his own apartment, I witness him receiving a letter that states that he cannot get an Arizona Driver License until he pays a fine for an abandoned vehicle of his that had been found on January 22nd.

John only speaks English, and he tells me at one point of time that since he has not learned Spanish yet, he probably never will. He uses me as a translator, but still seems to have an interest in learning at least a little Spanish as he repeatedly asks me what various items are called in Spanish.

John first moves into number 13, but is subsequently moved into number five, and Art takes over number 13. Then John gets his own apartment where he stays for most of the time.

Leaving Town

A few months later, John plans to leave for New York City (see also p. 52), and so the night before John takes the bus for Tucson, I ride by his apartment just to say good-bye. He is standing naked in the doorway and has packed everything up he needs, he tells me. He has also packed away his alarm clock, so he has no way of getting up as to make it for the first shuttle to Tucson, so he asks me to come by and wake him up at 5am. When I come by the next morning, he has already made some coffee and asks me to drink some with him before we leave for the bus station. We walk his things along Pan American Highway and he tells me he wants to get one last burrito before leaving. After getting the last two burritos at the Border Mart, we watch Mexican morning television at the bus station. While John is in the restroom, a man from further South in Mexico who has been studying English asks me whether John is my father.

It is not the only time that happens, and during John's time in Douglas, we spend a fair amount of time together.

Angel

Angel lives in #8 at the Lerman and has been doing so for the past 5 years, according to Mr. Fernandez. It's not quite clear how old he is, but my estimate is around 45, even though all his hair is still black.

In the Lerman, Angel is known for purchasing extra Food both through Food Stamps and the Food Bank and then selling it to others for a profit. Also, according to Mr. Fernandez, Angel will take and sell any shampoo left in the showers at the Lerman. I personally never have caught him or anyone else taking my shampoo, but I can confirm that shampoo disappears very fast around there.

Angel does help me fix my bicycle when I need to fix my tubes, and he first asks for a payment of 5 USD after he finishes the job, but the employee at the bicycle shop talks him down to 2 USD.

Angel only speaks Spanish, and his communication with John and the other English-only speakers is therefore somewhat limited.

When my bike gets stolen during one of the last days of my stay at the Lerman, John walks me to the police station. He is convinced that Zack instructed Angel to steal it. Angel later tells me that he has a collection of 23 to 33 bikes (the number varies), and he constantly comes home with yet another bike that he carries up the stairs of the Lerman and places inside his room. At the Lerman, Angel is staying in number eight. However, he moves out during my time in Douglas.

Zack

Zack is from Douglas, but has been in prison for running large amounts of drugs and his home has been burned down in the meantime and therefore he has to stay at the Lerman. Zack is in his early thirties, and he arrives at the Posada Lerman on the 15th of January and leaves in early March. Zack is a Hispanic and he speaks both English and Spanish fluently. At the Lerman, Zack is staying in room number seven, but then is gone after the first few months. It is after the end of my first stay that I hear reports of him showing up again in various places, although I never get to see him again myself.

Photo: Johannes Wilm

Picture 21: Tom and Sarah in the July 4th parade

Tom

Tom is a retired teacher and postal worker, and he is the husband of the librarian Sarah.

He is mostly known for riding around town and to the neighboring towns on his bicycle, and although he has a stroke around February and everyone thinks he is about to die, he is right back on his bike when he comes back from his hospital stay in Tucson. In the beginning he is even carrying a backpack connected with a tube to his leg. Tom has two bike shirts that he is using most frequently. One has Danish flag and a copy of Bjarne Riis's on it. The other one has a big Mexican flag on it.

In the July 4th parade, the librarians, including Sarah and Tom, have started to participate in a bike parade. All the Cyber teens are either riding bikes or walking in the parade. While riding a tandem bicycle, Sarah is wearing a shirt that has some of the symbolism of the American flag, while Tom wears his Mexican flag shirt. Bruce and his brother, who is on a short visit from Tucson, make sure not to make too much out of the event and so Bruce wears a shirt that says "Italia", while his brother wears a plain white t-shirt. They also go back home before the fireworks go off, while the rest of the town seems to assemble in 8th Street Park, where the parade was previously.

Tom is probably one of the informants least satisfied the government of the country he lives in.

Oscar

Oscar does not live at the Lerman, but while I live there, he visits me frequently. Oscar was the student council president of the 1997–1998 school year at Douglas High School, which he proudly mentions a lot. This places him close to my age of 23. He meets me in the Douglas library at the computers and hands me a business card with a bulldog on it — representing Douglas High School football team. He has moved out and lives in a small house a few blocks from the library where he has a computer and a satellite TV installed.

Oscar has had an accident, which smashed one of his legs severely in 2001 and he has received a settlement from it. Some say that his ambition level was better suited to the way he was before the accident and he has changed somewhat. His idea of becoming President of the U.S. (see p. 95) began before that time though.

The night when I am about to create a web page for Art, Oscar comes in and sits on the bed observing, while getting to know Art. This gives him the idea to make a web page of all the former student council presidents from the early 1900s until now. The way I understand our conversation, I agree to help him set it up himself for free, but one day he comes to me and tells me to type all the descriptions in the year book of all the student council presidents from 1900 till 2004, and to design a logo which is supposed to consist of a turning 3D picture of three stone bulldogs holding a sign saying "DHS" (Douglas High School). I refuse to do it, but I offer my help to him to show him how to do it on his own. He wants none of that and announces that he will not be back. A few months later he starts talking to me again and he tells me that he has hired someone for 100 USD. "You could be the one earning that money right now," Oscar tells me, but we agree not to take the issue up again.

Cosmic Peter

Cosmic Peter is an old friend of Kevin's, and he seems to be about 68 years old.

Cosmic Peter is on a lifetime disability payment for being injured many years before, but he seems to be just fine now. He has come through Douglas twice now when he moves from Mexico to the U.S. in his pickup that is rebuilt as a camper. And I am there when he comes back. He stays for about 10 days on the El Espejo parking lot, and is planning to come through Douglas twice a year in the future.

A few days after we all have had a discussion at El Espejo on the subject of war (see p. 153), Peter comes over to my desk at El Espejo while I am typing an article and tells me that he is impressed on how I "picked right up on that." He asks about the stipend that I am on, and immediately asks me whether it is a lifetime payment that I am on or whether it is only temporary. I specify that it is the latter, and he seems somewhat astonished. He tells me that I should better try and get it to be a permanent arrangement. "You know, I don't want to see you running around as this fifty year old socialist computer guy."

The day after Peter leaves, Kevin tells me: "Yesterday he went with me to watch my girls play, and I asked him whether he would leave and he didn't say anything. And this morning he was gone." I do know that his escape was planned though, because I talked to Peter shortly before he was to watch the game. He said that he would not see me again before fall, when he plans on going back to Mexico.

At that time, I am back in Europe.

Edwin Ludszeweit

Edwin is known for his long beard and he is mostly retired, which places him somewhere in excess of 60 years of age.

Edwin joined the Army in order to be sent to Europe, but after he was in, they sent him to Korea. Edwin used his connections and got transferred to Germany where he started bike racing for the Army. Then later on he was sent to Vietnam, but did not have to shoot anyone before he was discharged. "No one can kill anyone without getting screwed up," Edwin comments. He believes that it is a bad idea to join the military currently.

Edwin's stepfather's father started the Douglas Drugstore in 1902, which prompted Edwin to visit Douglas for short stays in 1956 and 1959. After he was done with his military service in 1966, he came back to run the drug store as no one else in the family wanted to it take over. He then stayed for 3 1/2 years before he left again in order to study for both a bachelor's and a master's degree. He then ran the drugstore for a while, until they closed down in the eighties because the store needed to be remodeled, which would have been too expensive. This was shortly before Wal-Mart moved in and took over the market, so in Edwin's opinion they "were quite lucky."

Edwin first hears that I am German and so he throws a German word into the conversation every now and then. Edwin's first wife was from Munich and she moved back there with her children after their divorce, and Edwin also has ancestors from Germany. Edwin seems to feel that the two of us have a common German-ness and more than once he ends a discussion with a statement that we both agree on: "And see, people here don't understand this." When he hears about me from Art, who talks about "the Swedish computer technician", he says to me the next time: "I didn't know you were just an ausländer[2]." He does it not in a negative manner though.

At one time Edwin wants me to put Linux on one of his old laptops, which I agree to do. Around the same time, my sandals are about to fall apart and as Edwin has nice sandals, I ask him where he got them. Edwin takes this as a sign of German-ness, and he immediately understands that I, as a fellow German, need

---

[2]'Ausländer' is German for foreigner.

comfortable sandals: "I used to order my sandals from Germany, but then Wal-Mart got these a couple of years ago. [...] I can find out whether they still have them." The next day, when Edwin pulls his pickup up at the library, he calls out of the window for me to "get on in." We drive to Wal-Mart, and Edwin shows me the same type of sandals that he has himself. I take them, and at the counter Edwin pays: "Oh, don't think about it after all the stuff you are doing for me with the Linux."

Back at the library, Art sits with Stan at computer #10, when we enter. He sees my new sandals and when I tell him Edwin bought them, he exclaims: "Oh, the old bartering system! Yeah, we need to bring that back," although he himself has been involved in quite a lot of bartering himself. Art wants my old sandals to use as a part to build an airplane with.

Edwin seems to be around most places I go most of the time, and when I am in Europe he keeps in contact. When I am back in Douglas for the second time, he helps me to arrange an airplane ticket to Brazil, although I would imagine that he is rather critical of my politics.

Maria & her crew

Maria is a high school graduate, but she is a little older than most other kids I meet.

One of the things I always wanted to do was to go "across the line" with some of these Douglas kids. Unfortunately it never happens. One of the main reasons is probably that Maria and her friends are considerably younger than me. Although several of them seem to treat me as if I was their age, inviting me for movie nights or to play computer games for hours on end, there is definitely a limit to my ability as a 23 year old, in terms of cruising for hours, followed by more hours of drinking and Playstation game playing. Therefore, my party coolness" status falls to "lame" pretty early on, after starting to hang with the main group and so crossing the line with them never happens.

Nevertheless, I do hang around them for long enough to hear what some of their motivations to go to Mexico are. While drinking

is not legal in the U.S. for anyone under 21, the legal age is 16 in
Agua Prieta. This means that all the young people have to go across
the line in order to drink legally. On top of that, the city of Douglas
has imposed a curfew at 10pm all weekend, so once the kids have
crossed the line, they will have to stay there until 6am the next
morning. Therefore the kids have to cross the line right at ten and
go cruising in Agua Prieta for a few hours before they hit the clubs.

One girl I talk to at the Dean campaign headquarters asks me
whether I have ever thought about getting myself pierced. Bruce is
walking a few feet behind me, and he almost chokes when he hears
the question and my surprised "no!" as an answer. She explains
that they use the time after they leave the clubs in Agua Prieta in
some abandoned houses piercing themselves and their friends.

The group that I get the closest to actually crossing with is a
group of kids that mostly are about to graduate from high school.
Maria is a 20-year-old high school graduate who works at the
library. She is of Mexican descent, but all her family has lived in
Douglas for generations. She works at the library and earns 110
USD a week as a part timer (19.5h) without health insurance. Out
of this Maria finances her V8 truck "Stevie," of which the down
payment alone is 80 USD every 2 weeks. The remaining dollars
go to a large extent into gas and some for alcohol. The back of the
pickup is mostly just for looks since Maria admits that she never
really uses it: "Except once, I found a dog in the middle of the street
and I picked it up and put it back there."

I have only spoken briefly to Maria at the library while checking
out books, when she tells one of the younger kids who hang around
there to tell me to show up at the school auditorium that night for
a concert. I do not quite know what to expect, and when I show
up it is during the last performance of the school orchestra when I
recognize her, her friend Robin and Adrian who I had seen around
8th Street Park before, both of them also in this year's graduating
class.

Soon thereafter I am invited on the trip to Sierra Vista. The next
morning I show up outside the library where Maria waits in her
truck "Stevie" and we first go to pick up Robin who lives outside of
town towards Sierra Vista. Maria has told everybody to bring their
music, as she is very concerned that I might not like any of their

particular music styles. Robin's father reminds me to "keep [my] hands to [my]self" before we drive off — he does not know that his 17 year old daughter recently discovered that she is a lesbian. After going back to Douglas and picking up a third young man Carmelo, and using up some time driving around, we are finally on our way to Sierra Vista. There we are heading straight for the mall where some of their high school friends, including Adrian, wait. We hang around there for a while before we go on to the tattoo shop where one of the girls plans to get a tattoo and then on to the piercing shop where Adrian is to get his lip pierced. After the tattoo and piercing, we go to a bookstore to read sex horoscopes aloud and then to a burger place before we go back to Douglas again. "You spend so much money every time you are in Sierra Vista cause there are so many cool things you can buy," Robin, who defines herself to a large extent around listening to punk music, exclaims when calculations are made of how much money each one spent that day.

That evening I end up hanging around Maria, Robin and her girlfriend Rosa out at a lake. A few days later, Rosa breaks up with Robin, and Robin is suddenly not so sure about being lesbian any more. Robin's last boyfriend was Carmelo and she cheated on him with Rosa. Rosa has known that she is lesbian since she was 6, and a few days after breaking up with Robin, Robin's openly lesbian sister Nay comes back from California where she has stayed with family for some time, and Rosa says she is in love with her. They never get together though, and instead Rosa falls in love with a boy, James, who also is one of Maria's close friends. Maria has also been together with both Carmelo and Nay before, and Nay and Carmelo have also been together at one point of time. Nay explains the complicated nature of their relationships: "In Douglas every guy will go sleep with another guy at least once, just to see what it is like." And Maria adds: "See a Douglas relationship never lasts, and everybody knows that."

Art

Art is around 55, and I get into contact with him when he decides to introduce himself while we are waiting for the library to open one Saturday in January. Then he goes in and talks without break until the library closes that day — about Adam Smith, how Linux will revolutionize the world, etc. At the Lerman, Art first moved into number 13, and when John moves out, he is transferred to number five.

Art has been going around for most of his life without much money. When I arrive in Douglas, he has been living on and off in his car for the past 2–3 years whenever he cannot find a place in a shelter.

Art lives in the same rooms as John, but that is because he moves in later than John and he can therefore take over the rooms in the order that John vacates them. Art has educated himself through libraries and he has held various jobs over the years that brought him close to engineering although he never had any formal education beyond high school. I see him for several days when he lives in his car in the parking lot outside the library without talking to him. He is known by the Cyber teens as the "Californian" simply for his way of being. It is also true that he has been living in California for most of his adult life, but he originally came from Texas.

Art's initial plan when I meet him is to set up a grinding class for telescope lenses. Art has designed his own telescope using a "folded Newtonian design". He has built all the parts and has stored them away in the trunk of his car. All one needs for grinding lenses is "an old washing machine, so tell me if you see one," he explains. After a few weeks we talk about the possibility of setting up a web page describing his design, which he tells me is quite revolutionary. He would like to sell different telescope parts over the web. I offer my help and a few days later I sit at the Lerman hotel with my laptop that I had been hiding under my clothing, while Art sits on the bed and dictates what he wants on the page. He also has a picture of him holding the telescope that he made at a shelter (his car is in the background) further up North where he was staying for a while, and another one showing all the individual components. I put all that together and the next day I put it on my university web space.

In order to promote his page, I suggest to him that we submit it to Slashdot.org[3]. A few days later, Slashdot.org actually accepts the "news" onto their site:

> Folded Newtonian Telescope
>
> johanneswilm writes *"Arthur Caveny has figured out a way to overcome many of the problems of traditional telescope construction — making it way more compact and economical. And the whole thing is completely portable and achieves accuracy down to one or two millionths of an inch across an 18 inch surface!"*

It is the most impressive sounding abstract Art is able to produce and it gets him in. "This is it!" Art exclaims after he notices that some hundreds or thousands have visited his site and left a comment in the Slashdot forum. He is sure that he will now be famous and never again have to sleep in his car. And indeed, he does get an e-mail from a Michael Hopkin of *Nature Magazine*[4] asking what was so revolutionary about his telescope as well as an e-mail from a publisher who wants to strike a deal with him about writing a book on it. Art does not see any reason to answer most of the e-mails that are only concerned about minor points and where he feels that he can clearly tell that they do not really understand even the "most basic principles of telescoping."

He does look at answering the e-mail from the publisher and the reporter though. To the reporter he writes, quite honestly, that there are no revolutionary new things in his telescope and that he only combines inventions that have been made over the last 30 years and that have been forgotten over the years. He never hears from the reporter again. He does have a longer exchange with the publisher though. The publisher wants to know what Art has to offer exactly in terms of plans, and to either call him or give him his phone number. Art is afraid that he might find out that he lives

---

[3]Slashdot.org is a pretty well-known general tech site that it is very hard to get accepted to.

[4]*Nature Magazine* is a rather famous magazine on natural science.

in his car and so he thinks of ways of getting a hold of a phone number that the publisher can call without making it apparent that he does not have a real home. I am acting as Art's secretary, since he cannot type very fast. I suggest to him that he should try to get a cell phone without monthly payments, because I know they are cheap in Europe. He checks the prices and finds they are out of his price range. Instead he talks a lady he knows from church into lending him her mobile phone for a day when he asks the publisher to call him.

The next problem for Art is payment. The publisher gives Art two different options: either he pays them for the printing and he will get all the profits himself, or they pay the printing expenses and he will get a certain percentage of the profit. Art needs them to pay some money in advance though, as he does not have any money to start out with. It drags on for a few weeks and Art finally seems to get a deal so he talks Oscar into typing the book for him. Art wants to borrow my recording device at first so that he can record what he wants typed and Oscar can then type it later on, but after their first session, Art returns the device and tells me that they are working fine without the recorder and that he has told Oscar a lot of information that he will type that night at home. The next day, Art is eager to continue dictating, but Oscar says he wants to wait till Friday. And on the coming Friday, he wants to wait some time longer. They never get to do another session, and Art's book project never materializes.

Stan

Stan is an ex computer programmer and database manager from Santa Cruz, who bought 40 acres of land close to Douglas when he was still employed. He now wants to start a sustainable community there, which will be off the grid and will grow fruits and vegetables. He seems to be in the same age group as Art. He made some risky investments in offshore ventures and lost most of his money, although he tells me that he might get "half a million back" soon. He has stored away all the money he has left in gold coins so the government will not to be able to track it, because the Internal

Revenue Service (IRS)[5] is auditing him and because he "doesn't believe in keeping money in FDIC banks"[6]. Stan does not believe today's problems are due to capitalism in itself. Also for him, the problem lies in the way monopolism has been able to take over. So when I talk about exploitation by employers, he responds "don't forget the interest on the national debt, requiring much higher income tax than necessary, and the fact that those interest payments go to private parties, the owners of the 'Federal' Reserve Banks." As he sees it, "IRS Agents are collection agents for monopolistic corporations with government contracts and for the private owners of the F[ederal] R[eserve] Banks."

After I have left the first time, he lets Art move out with him. Stan lives in a motor home that no longer runs that he got for free, and survives by being frugal and selling a coin or two when he needs to. He gets most of his food from the Douglas Food Bank, the 'Red and White' store which sells expired items at a steep discount, and his garden. Art lives in one of the campers near Stan's motor home and gets by on his food stamps and occasional bartering and odd jobs.

Todd

Todd is in his fifties and I move in with Todd after staying in the Lerman for about a month. At his place, we both sleep in sleeping bags on cots in the basement, as he does not have any furniture and does not want to spend money on fixing the heating system.

I meet Todd initially at a Howard Dean campaign meeting. Bruce has invited me to go door to door for the Dean campaign, but first we meet up at a local workers' club. The Barkers drive over to the bakery La Gardin for coffee and offer Todd a ride, but he is concerned that he might spill the coffee and so he walks instead. Our candidate is almost out of the race at this moment because he held a speech after losing the primaries in Iowa where he lost his

---

[5]The IRS is the US government agency responsible for tax collection and tax law enforcement.

[6]FDIC banks are banks insured through the Federal Deposit Insurance Corporation (FDIC).

Photo: Johannes Wilm

Picture 22: Kids playing soccer on the parking lot in front of Todd's house and behind La Gardin

voice and ends his speech with a "yehaa!" scream. Apparently that disqualifies him from being the next U.S. President; at least that is what the major networks think as they are playing the clip over and over again. Therefore, at the meeting we first get to see a presentation on a laptop of how the news media is using it as propaganda in order to get him out of the race. Then we go for a presentation round. The local campaign manager presents me as "Johaans from Denmark", and when it is Todd's turn to present himself, he presents himself as Todd from "Dogpatch". In the coming month, "Dogpatch" first changes into "Dogwater" and finally, when it seems more and more unlikely that Todd will get a job around Douglas, it changes into "Dogass."

I walk around with Bruce that day and only see Todd briefly after we have been going on our rounds, when Bruce introduces me as a politically-aware anthropologist from Norway. Todd himself holds a master's degree in anthropology from the University of Montana, he tells me later on.

A few days later, I hear from Sarah that Todd has been calling the library in order to get hold of me, and that he wants me to come over there. I do not get to go to El Espejo where he hangs out all day right then, but from Bruce I hear that the purpose of his attempts to contact me is to offer me to stay in his house, which is only a block away from the library, on the opposite side of where the Lerman is. Todd keeps on calling for another day or so and finally I do go over there. We walk to his house and he tries to show all the worst things about it to begin with — including the furniture issue. It used to be a doctor's office, so the lighting is fluorescent, the kitchen table is messy and there is ice growing out of a fridge that is the size of a microwave, one has to turn the main faucet in the house on before one can use the tap in the bathroom, while the sink in the kitchen is not altogether unusable.

I tell Todd that I would very much like to move there, and he answers with an astonished "huh." But we agree on it, and I get to move there a few days later just before Todd gets his job outside of town, which means that he will only be home during the weekends.

Kevin

Kevin also seems to be in his fifties, and he had been a journalist for the New York Times at some point of time. In the eighties, he was working at a newspaper and was assigned to write about the Mexican elections. He wanted to go to Hermosillo, the capital of the state of Sonora, but they send him to Agua Prieta instead. It so happened that after the elections, riots erupted in Agua Prieta because the government was accused of fraud. The federal Mexican army was sent in and Kevin therefore had to stay somewhat longer. During that time, he noticed that there was an apparent lack of juice bars as he had seen in other Mexican cities, and so he set one up in Agua Prieta. Later he wrote an article on how a certain baking ingredient that many choose to buy in Mexico because it is so much cheaper, was so cheap because it was produced chemically and that it was dangerous for one's health. For the article he needed a person to hold the ingredient, and the woman he found for it later became his wife.

He now has five kids with his wife and they live together just across the border in a house built ecologically correct. According to Kevin, they built it there because it would not have to conform to the strict building codes that the U.S. has in effect.

Kevin dislikes the more commercialized and streamlined parts of culture one can find in America. He thinks very little of Southern California and big cities in other places that have a very commercial flair to them. He is therefore very frustrated that the goal of many in Douglas is exactly to go to these places: "It's always Disneyland or Las Vegas and people get real excited about it."

As El Espejo just makes a few dollars a day, and Kevin's income from the adoptions and occasional newspaper jobs appear to amount to very little, it is generally held that Kevin has income from some other source to finance his kids and wife. Some rumors place him on the pay-role of either drug dealers or some federal undercover agency, and others believe he is dependent on his mother. He is also still doing small jobs for different media companies when they need a story on the border.

Garry Mora

Garry Mora is the owner of California Pizza and he is Korean. He got American citizenship by fighting in the Vietnam War. He also earns extra income by loaning out money for very high interest. He has two teen-age kids and is in his fifties.

I meet Garry Mora soon after I arrive when I do not yet have any daily routines or eating arrangements with anyone, so by default I dine at his "all you can eat" pizza buffet. Garry Mora has been working "very hard" all his life, he explains. Garry Mora sees the two of us having a commonality, because we are neither American nor Mexican.

Bicycle Peter

Bicycle Peter is originally from Houston, Texas and he was in the Korean War, which places him in his sixties or seventies. He joined the Marine Corps, because his dad had done so, and not for an

Photo: Johannes Wilm

Picture 23: Douglas is still wealthy compared to Agua Prieta.

"economic reason," he tells me. For training they went to California, and on the way through they stopped in Douglas. That was when Peter saw Douglas for the very first time. In the Korean War he was injured, and transferred to Japan, where he was put on embassy duty in Tokyo after getting out of the hospital.

I first meet Bicycle Peter at El Espejo. Kevin tells me he knows about a man who has connections to a woman doing sewing jobs when I have a ripped jacket. Bicycle Peter comes to El Espejo a little while afterwards and I am introduced as an anthropologist from Norway. Kevin gives him a free drink and afterwards we go over to the woman's place. She lives only two blocks away and I am asked to sit in the sofa while she does the job. Peter walks off doing some other chores, leaving me with her for a while. She only speaks Spanish, but she has an English sign posted on her door, which says her daughter made the honor roll.

Later I learn that she is one of three women who Peter has helped to get across the border.

Sgt. Skinner

One recruiter stands out, since he is known by name by the younger informants. My estimate is that he is in his thirties or forties. I meet him when I still have my own bike. There is a hole in one of the tires one day, so I put the bike upside down outside the library. First Sarah comes by and it is the way I first meet her. But then a few minutes later another guy pulls up in the parking lot — an ARMY recruiter. Sgt. Skinner does not wear his uniform that day and he walks straight over to my bike: "What has happened?" I tell him that there is a hole in the tire and he asks me whether I am from around here. I tell him, that I am from Europe, and he asks again, whether I am from Germany. "Yeah, also," I reply to cut the conversation short. "Ich bin aus Idar Oberstein,"[7] Sgt. Jürgen Skinner surprises me by speaking completely accent-free German. He asks whether I am on a bike trip around Mexico or the U.S., and when I tell him that I am to live there for six months, he replies: "Das schaffst du nie."[8] and invites me to visit him in Sierra Vista.

While we still sit there with the bike, Bill, who works at the library, walks by and says: "Hey, where is the uniform, Sgt. Skinner?" Within a split second, Sgt. Skinner turns into the most "American" American I have ever met and while jumping towards Bill, replies "Hey Biiiiill, you know the drill, it's suits on Friiiidays, you know the drill" and he runs off into the library. Once inside, Sgt. Skinner starts talking to two young potential recruits.

He comes back many times.

---

[7]"I am from Idar Oberstein." — in Bavaria, Germany
[8]"You're never going to make it."

Appendix B

History, Terms, Tools & Problems

History

Douglas was founded in 1901 as a smelter town for the copper mine in nearby Bisbee. Up until the 1980s the smelter operated and almost all employment in the town was provided by the company that operated both the mine and the smelter, Phelps Dodge. In the early eighties, the Anglo management of the smelter was moved to Phoenix, and a few years later the smelter was closed completely. Many blame environmentalists for implementing standards that were too high, but at the same time Phelps Dodge's move to relocate to a cheaper location in Mexico was occurring frequently for other businesses in that period as well.

At the same time, industrialism has steadily declined as productivity of workers has gone up, and as Mike Davis (2004, 10) explains, most new cities nowadays are no longer resembling Manchester, Berlin and Chicago in their built-up areas, but rather Dublin between 1800–1850, which suffered from de-industrialization. Although Davis' scope of his description is the 'global south' (somewhat vaguely defined as most of Africa, South and Central America and great parts of Asia), Douglas very much falls into the same category of a de-industrialized city that now only contains one huge lumpenproletariat.

Photo: Johannes Wilm

Picture 24: Douglas' low altitude made it the perfect location for a smelter.

Neighboring Agua Prieta looks even worse, although there actually are some industrial jobs left. While Agua Prieta historically was about equal to the size of Douglas, recently it has grown to somewhere above 150,000 people with Douglas, although slowly growing, remaining at a level below 20,000. It almost entirely consists of slums, but as Davis points out, these modern-day slums are not in the inner city but rather on the outskirts (Davis 2004, 14).

Although highly segregated, the twin cities of Douglas and Agua Prieta meant a higher standard of living for many newcomers during the Phelps Dodge era. Now though, exactly following the pattern that Davis draws, the city no longer stands for progress and increasing living standards, but rather for unprotected work and a growing informal sector (Davis 2004, 23).

But with all the similarities to some poorer areas of Europe, there are at least two big differences. One factor is that there is no way to escape the situation by moving geographically, as it had been for many Irish by going to the United States had during Marx's time (Davis 2004, 28). This becomes especially apparent in

Photo: Johannes Wilm

Picture 25: A closed down business — one of many

Douglas, as Agua Prieta is for many the Promised Land that the road that was supposed to lead them to, but whose doors were closed for them. The other difference is that while moving to the city meant secularizing in Marx's time, today various fanatical Christian groups have taken the position once held by socialist and anarchist groups in organizing urban newcomers (Davis 2004, 30). Also this is consistent in both Douglas and Agua Prieta where posters for such groups dominated, and even those Douglas kids who have graduated from high school were caught in various inner-religious discussions. But as one can read in the chapter on war and nationalism, many have not turned quite as anti-revolutionary as Davis predicts.

Terminology

There are three main terms that I have used, which I felt were too complicated to explain in the text itself without hurting the general flow. I have instead decided to include them here.

Photo: Johannes Wilm

Picture 26: Collection for veterans during the annual "Arts in the Park"

The idea of a dual notion of nationalism under capitalism

Avineri (1991) tries to give an answer to the two contradictory ideas of nationalism in Marx's writings. On the one hand, Marx described capitalism in the communist manifesto as spreading across national boundaries rapidly and as having an immensely homogenizing effect on the peoples it encountered (Avineri 1991, 639). On the other hand, nationalist movements gained immensely in power from 1848 onwards, and so Marx revised his position. Nationalism was to be seen as a necessary part of the superstructure of capitalist society (Avineri 1991, 640–641). Avineri sees these two ideas of nationalism as a contradiction within Marxism — but they can equally well be seen as complementary to one another.

The concept of citizenship

One of the ideas that I believe comes naturally and that I have chosen to focus on when looking at borders is the concept of citizenship — a rather recent phenomenon that has come with advent of the concept of nations, which in turn came about with the introduction of capitalism (Hobsbawm 1990) or industrialism (Gellner 1983) — both ideas fitting very well within a Marxist framework. Before, the people in the sphere of influence of some monarch or in some feudal system did not necessarily have a homogeneous culture, and rights and duties were also not automatically given out evenly to the inhabitants of a certain area. One of the main events that changed this was the invention of the printing press, which made it possible for the people of an area too large for everyone to know each other personally to read the same Latin books. And when the market for the Latin readership was saturated, the market for printed books tried to conquer new markets and 'invented' certain standardizations of oral languages, which lead to the development of national cultures (Anderson 1994, 90). Another main event was the industrial revolution, as industrial capitalism required a standardized, exchangeable work force so that wages would be nothing but a calculation that could be scaled upwards indefinitely without having to consider any specialized skills of the individual worker (Hobsbawm 1990) and for that purpose they supported creating national school systems.

The homogenization within single countries led to the appearance of borders to not only separate the sphere of influence of different states, but also to separate people on the basis of language, culture and income (Scott 1998). The institution of citizenship was invented on top of that. The individual suddenly had certain rights, such as schooling in the local public system, but also certain duties for this country, such as military service and respect for the laws governing it (Scott 1998). However, as Billig (1995) notes, the existence of nations has to be reinforced, since it cannot be taken as a given that nations continue to exist as a mere function of their historic creation. Hobsbawm (1990) adds that members of the society might not give top priority to the importance of the national identity at all times, despite what national leaders, who have a self-interest in the continued existence of the nation, might say.

In most places, the conformity to the duties laid upon citizens by the state will be maintained by the combination of direct law enforcement by the state and by a nationalistic ideology that it is right to follow the conventions imposed by the state. However, it will be hard to predict the degree to which the state keeps its power as a result of either of the two.

In border towns however, the possibility of gaining at least some of the rights of either country while avoiding the duties of either always exists. Therefore in border towns, the degree to which the laws of the countries are respected depends to a much larger extent on the strength of nationalist ideology.

The term 'lumpenproletariat'

The term 'lumpenproletariat' is a Marxist term and generally denotes a segment of the population that is neither working nor has the wealth to own any means of production themselves. Today, Marxists usually denote unemployed people with this term, and that makes it relevant for studying Douglas. However, its usage in the classical Marxist literature was not only a definition of the members of the lumpenproletariat, but also a statement about their role in modern day history. In 1849, Engels writes:

> The Swiss proletariat is still largely what one describes as lumpenproletariat, prepared to sell themselves to anyone who will make extravagant promises. (Engels 1849)

Two decades later, in 1870, Engels' use of the term has shifted somewhat:

> The lumpenproletariat, this scum of the decaying elements of all classes, which establishes headquarters in all the big cities, is the worst of all possible allies. [...] If the French workers, in the course of the Revolution, inscribed on the houses: Mort aux voleurs![1] and even shot down many, they did it, not out of enthusiasm for property, but because they rightly considered it necessary to hold that band at arm's length. Every leader of the workers who utilizes these gutter-proletarians as guards or supports, proves himself by this action

---

[1]"Death to the thieves!"

alone a traitor to the movement. (Engels 1870, author's preface)

While the first use of the term implies that the lumpenproletariat simply is a proletariat on a lower stage of development, the latter use implies that it is a group of unemployed or semi-employed, who co-exists with the proletariat, but they are unreliable as revolutionary agents because their ideologies are unpredictable and they can be mobilized by either side in the class struggle between bourgeoisie and proper proletariat.

It is the latter that has become the most common use in the post-Marx era, and it is also the version of the term that is useful here to describe a large part of the Douglas population, which is either always out of work, or works very little. However, question of what the lumpenproletariat's role is nowadays can probably not be answered this easily, but the reader may make his or her own conclusions while examining the various cases presented here.

Theoretical Tools

How the field work was conducted
    The data collection has been done in mostly three ways:

1. Taking notes of a day's events in the evening.

2. Recording conversations of informants on tape.

3. Sending and receiving electronic messages.

Now these three ways also have internal subgroups. The recordings of daily events, which I did mostly during the first 1–2 months, sometimes take the form of writing down quotes of what informants said almost verbatim, and sometimes just reciting events. I resorted to recording informants on tape because I wanted to have more accurate quotes from informants that. It took both the form of formal interviews, which still were mainly controlled by the person being interviewed, and of recording informal conversation. Nevertheless, except for the interview with Alexis Sanders, the candidate for mayor, and a rather informal interview with Bob Waczkovic

Photo: Johannes Wilm

Picture 27: The new Wal-Mart Superstore is the subject of many conversations.

and Garst Williams from the gun shop, all of the interviews had been preceded by a time when I got acquainted with my interview partner in a more informal setting, so they knew I sympathized with them at least on some level. That gave them some leeway in the way they framed their answers.

The third method of electronic communication included sending e-mails to either others or myself. It is what replaced my daily notes after the initial 1–2 months for several reasons. E-mailed notes would already be typed out, and they would already be in Norway in a convenient electronic form when I got back. As it turned out that just about everyone is involved in so-called "crime" in Douglas, I was not sure whether it was smart either to take the material through customs or to send it by traditional mail. Also, it gave me an excuse to hang around the library more often without looking as though I was doing nothing. At the same time, especially the youths all had e-mail and instant messaging so I received quite a bit of information by communication with them electronically as well.

My main theoretical approach was to participate and help in the daily life of people in Douglas. Several people had computer problems that I could fix, the library had several younger teenagers who needed help with homework, one man needed help preparing his tax return, the Douglas Democrats needed help in their campaigns (the great majority of Douglas is Democratic, but still I did get to talk to Republicans as well), one man needed to get his yard cleaned because someone had burned his house down while he was in prison, one person needed extensive plumbing done in his house, a scientist needed to get off the street and get his ideas sent to others over the Internet, one older man tried to get a prostitute to move close to the border so he could send her child to school and therefore was in need of small sums of money, the librarian's son who had recently come back from after studying and working in Europe needed someone from Europe to talk to, and some conservative youths wanted to discuss politics with me.

It is in this way that I won the trust of my informants, and most information I received I only got because they saw me more like just another youngster in town than a person from university. At least that was my perception at the time. I did always mention where I came from and what I was doing, but most did not spend much time worrying about it. One man even responded by telling me he really was a millionaire — he believed the thing about me studying at a university simply to be my "story."

Problematic Issues

There are several problematic aspects with this study.

Sample

First of all, Douglas should have approximately 1960 non-Hispanic inhabitants, while I have only spoken to a small fraction of these. And the number of people I have had close contact with is even smaller. According to Jeff I have picked a rather skewed sample:

Picture 28: The area where the Barkers live is somewhat wealthier.

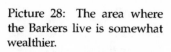

Photo: Johannes Wilm

> You brought your predetermined views to the U.S., you surrounded yourself with people of relatively the same views, and now you've left with he same view.

Jeff is right about the fact that my view of the current U.S. foreign policy has not changed radically. And also, the collaboration in the Dean campaign meant that I came into contact with Todd and through him with Kevin and a network of others. Nevertheless, I did also get into contact with Jeff and January, the guys running the gun shop, and also Lou at the Douglas museum who were all outspokenly Republicans. I also do have major differences in opinions with John, Zack, Angel, Lisa or many others who I nevertheless talked to and questioned for their opinions on various matters.

Therefore, I believe Jeff's statement is more a reflection of his own frustration of not having been able to change my opinion on a range of issues than a neutral assessment that I have only surrounded myself by like-minded people.

It is true nevertheless that my sample is skewed, and it particularly favors people who are active in public life in public institutions other than the schools, as these were easier accessible for an outsider. My conclusions therefore cannot be taken as proven facts that hold true for society at large, but rather as ideas that have some truth in them, and there is no concrete reason for me to expect that other parts of society are very much different.

Some also say that I misrepresent in that I do not look very much at wealthy Douglasites. However, if I misrepresent, I'd rather say it's the other way round: those I have not talked to are those Mexican workers who freeze to death in a ditch while hiding from the border patrols. And about the rich: well, I really don't care much about them, and I don't see much point in studying how they live if it is not about showing the contrast to ordinary people, as their wealth is built on the back of those they exploited.

Time slices

Another problem is that those I did speak to, I only saw during certain times of the day. Although I could come by El Espejo during the daytime and Kevin would mostly be there, he also spent time with his children going to various sports with them, and he had a house across the line. I did not see the house before my second visit, and I only saw him and his family riding by at various times when they were off to some sporting event. I never got to know where the gun shop people live, and I would only meet the people around the Douglas Wendt in that setting as being part of the staff there or occasionally at Food City or Safeway.

The problem of only having access to people during certain time slices is something every anthropologist studying modern societies will encounter, because people are only available at certain times and are not able to devote all their time to the anthropologist, and they also don't want him to see them in all situations. This makes it somewhat hard to interpret their particular way of enacting what Goffman calls impression management (Goffman 1959, 208).

Nevertheless, I do believe that the problem is not as big as it would be studying other places. The high unemployment rate means that many actually do have a lot of time, and I am able to account for nearly all times of the day in the life of John, Art and the others from the Lerman as well as the Barkers and Todd. Comparatively, the amount of different personas one can present to different groups is also limited, because word of mouth spreads quickly in such a small town. At times, I overestimate this though. Particularly the youths are not be too well connected with one another, or at least they pretend not to be. For instances, after I meet David and I go to his party, January, Lisa and Jeff meet me at the library a few days later. I tell them the story, and they say they "probably" know which David I am talking about. A few days later, January and Lisa tell me they talked to the person they thought I was referring to but it was not the right one.

To me this seems strange, because I see David all the time at various places in town, and I have a hard time imagining all the teenagers do not know one another pretty intimately.

Bibliography

Acton, Edward. *Rethinking the Russian Revolution*. London: Arnold, 1990.

Alonso, Ana Maria. "The Politics of Space, Time and Substance: State Formation, Nationalism and Ethnicity." *Annual Review of Anthropology* 23 (1994): 379–405.

Alvarez, Robert R.,Jr. "The Mexican-US Border: The Making of an Anthropology of Borderlands." *Annual Review of Anthropology* 24 (1995): 447–470.

Amin, Samir. "Self-reliance and the New International Economic Order." *Transforming the World-Economy? Nine Critical Essays on the New International Economic Order*. Ed. Herb Addo. Hodder and Stoughton, 1984. 204–219.

Anderson, Benedict. *Imagined Communities: Reflections on the Origin and Spread of Nationalism*. Revised edition. London: Verso, 1991.

Anderson, Benedict. "Imagined Communities." *Nationalism*. Oxford: Oxford University Press. 1994.

Anderson, Nels. *The Hobo*. Chicago: The University of Chicago Press, 1923.

Avineri, Shlomo. "Marxism and Nationalism." *Journalism and Contemporary History* 26 (1991): 637–657.

Barth, Frederik. "Introduction." *Ethnic Groups and Boundaries — The Social Organization of Culture Difference*, 3rd edition. Oslo: Universitetsforlaget. 1982.

Berthoud, Gerald and Fabrizio Sabelli. "Our Obsolete Production Mentality: The Heresy of the Communal Formation." *Current Anthropology* 20 (12 1979): 745–760.

Billig, Michael. *Banal Nationalism*. London: Sage Publications, 1995.

Bonnand, Sheila. *The Bisbee Deportation of 1917 — A University of Arizona Web Exhibit*. 1997. Available from: http://aquarius.library.arizona.edu/exhibits/bisbee/history/overview.html [cited November 27th 2005].

Boswell, Terry and William J. Dixon. "Marx's Theory of Rebellion: A Cross-National Analysis of Class Exploitation, Economic Development, and Violent Revolt." *American Sociological Review* 58 (10 1993): 681–702.

Bourdieu, Pierre *The Forms of Capital*. New York: Greenwood Press. 1986. 241–258.

Bourdieu, Pierre. *Distinction: A Social Critique of the Judgement of Taste*. Ed. Richard Nice. Reprint edition. Cambridge: Harvard University Press, 1987.

Brenner, Robert. *The Boom and The Bubble — The US in the World Economy*. London: Verso, 2002.

Census, US. "US Census 2000." (2000). Available from: http://en.wikipedia.org/wiki/Douglas,_Arizona [cited February 10th 2005].

Chambliss, William J. "Toward a Political Economy of Crime." *Theory and Society* 2 (1975): 149–170.

Colvin, Mark and John Pauly. "A Critique of Criminology: Toward an Integrated Structural-Marxist Theory of Delinquency Production." *The American Journal of Sociology* 89 (11 1983): 513–551.

Davis, Mike. "Planet of Slums." *New Left Review* 26 (3/4 2004): 5–34.

Donnan, Hastings and Thomas M. Wilson. *Borders: Frontiers of Identity, Nation and State*. Oxford and New York: Berg, 1999.

Ehrenreich, Barbara. *Nickel and Dimed — Undercover in Low-wage USA*. Great britain edition. 2/3 Hanover Yard, London N1 8BE: Granta, 2002.

Engels, Friedrich. "The Model Republic." *Neue Rheinische Zeitung* (March 15 1849). Available from: http://www.marxists. org/archive/marx/works/1849/03/11.htm [cited May 16th 2005].

Engels, Friedrich. *The Peasant War in Germany*. 2nd edition. London: Neue Rheinische Zeitung, 1870. Available from: http://www.marxists.org/archive/marx/works/ 1850/peasant-war-germany/ [cited May 16th 2005].

Engels, Friedrich and Karl Marx. *The German Ideology*. Ed. C.J Arthur. 2nd edition. Lawrence and Wishart, 1974.

Frank, Andre Gunder. "Development and Underdevelopment in the New World: Smith and Marx vs. the Weberians." *Theory and Society* 2 (1975): 431–466.

Frank, Andre Gunder. "The Development of Underdevelopment." *Development Studies. A Reader.*. Ed. Stuart Corbridge. Edward Arnold Publishers Ltd., 1995. chapter 2, 27–37.

Gellner, Ernest. *Nations and Nationalism*. Cornell University Press, 1983.

Glesne, Mark. *Military Missing Recruitment Quotas: Good For My Morale*. 2005. Available from: http://www. americandaily.com/article/7831 [cited May 22nd 2005].

Goffman, Erving. *The Presentation of Self in Everyday Life*. New York: Anchor, 1959.

Hall, Thomas D. "World-System Theory." *The Dictionary of Anthropology*. Oxford: Blackwell Publishers Ltd. 1997. 498–499.

Hobsbawm, Eric J. *Nations and Nationalism Since 1780*. Cambridge: Cambridge University Press, 1990.

Holdt, Jacob. *Amerikanske Bilder*. 3rd edition. Copenhagen: Pax Forlag, 1979. Available from: http: //www.american-pictures.com/.

Huntington, Samuel P. "The Hispanic Challenge." *Foreign Policy* March/April (2004). Available from: http://www.foreignpolicy.com/story/cms.php?story_id=2495&print=1 [cited February 10th 2005].

Jeffrey, Robert S. *The History of Douglas, Arizona*. s.n., 1951.

Marcus, Anthony. "The Culture of Poverty Revisited: Bringing Back the Working Class." *Anthropologica* 47 (2005): 35–52.

Marcus, Anthony and Charles Menzies. "Renewing the Vision: Marxism and Anthropology in the 21st Century — Introduction." *Anthropologica* 47 (2005): 3–6.

Marcus, Anthony and Charles Menzies. "Towards a Class-Struggle Anthropology." *Anthropologica* 47 (2005): 13–33.

Marx, Karl. *The Difference Between the Democritean and Epicurean Philosophy of Nature*. PhD thesis, Humboldt, Berlin, March 1841.

Marx, Karl. *Capital — A new abridgement*. Ed. David McLellan. Oxford University Press, 1999.

Miller, Tom. *On the Border: Portraits of America's Southwestern Frontier*. Lincoln, NE: iUniverse.com, Inc., 2000.

Neale, Jonathan. *What's Wrong with America? — How the rich and powerful have changed America and now want to change the world*. London: Vision Paperbacks, 2004.

Commerce Communications Division, Arizona Departmentof. Douglas Community Profile. Technical report, Arizona Department of Commerce, Douglas, June 2005. Available from: http://www.azcommerce.com/doclib/commune/douglas.pdf.

Offman, Craig. "The 10 Most Corrupt Cities in America." *George Magazine* (March 1998).

O'Laughlin, Bridget. "Marxist Approaches in Anthropology." *Annual Review of Anthropology* 4 (1975): 341–370.

Roseberry, William. "Marxist Anthropology." *The Dictionary of Anthropology*. Oxford: Blackwell Publishers Ltd. 1997. 307–309.

Roseberry, William. "Marx and Anthropology." *Annual Revew of Anthropology* 26 (1997): 25–46.

Schwarzenegger, Arnold. "Republican National Convention Address." 8 2004. Available from: `http://www.americanrhetoric.com/speeches/convention2004/arnoldschwarzenegger2004rnc.htm` [cited February 10th 2005].

Scott, James C. *Seeing Like A State*. New Haven: Yale University Press, 1998.

Smith, Adam. *The Wealth of Nations*. Penguin classics edition. London: Penguin Group, 1999.

Stern, Alexandra Minna. "Nationalism on the Line: Masculinity, Race, and the creation of the U.S. Border Patrol, 1910–1940." *Continental Crossroads — Remapping U.S.-Mexico Borderlands History*. Ed. Samuel Truett and Elliott Young. Durham and London: Duke University Press, 2004. 299–323.

Weisman, Alan. *La frontera — The United States Border with Mexico*. Tucson: The University of Arizona Press, 1986.

Whyte, William Foote. *Street Corner Society — The Social Structure of an Italian Slum*. 4th edition. Chicago: The University of Chicago Press, 1993.

Zaragoza, Xavier. "Record number of immigrants caught." *The Daily Dispatch* (October 5 2000).

Photo: Johannes Wilm

Picture 29: A few chain stores have been established west of town.

Photo: Johannes Wilm

Picture 30: A few miles outside of Douglas, the border fence suddenly ends.

Printed in the United States
64536LVS00003B/291